The Conversion of
Buster Drumwright

THE
CONVERSION
OF
Buster Drumwright

The television and stage scripts

Jesse Hill Ford

VANDERBILT

Nashville

1964

FOR
MY MOTHER AND FATHER

Preface

THE FIRST PLAY I wrote for television was *The Conversion of Buster Drumwright*. It may very well be my last, for the experience spoiled me.

After working with the CBS Television Workshop under Albert McCleery, the producer; with George Keathley, the director of the play; with Rosemary Foster, who, in her capacity as story editor, helped me to get the material organized before I wrote it; and with the associate producers, Ethel Frank and Victor Allan, I am not very much inclined to settle for less, and other production outfits to whom I have talked since then instinctively feel, I am sure, that I am spoiled. They are correct if they sense this.

The fact is that I had the best of everything: absolute freedom to write my own play in my own way and say-so in its casting. I was treated as a playwright, not as a hack writer consigned to his stable. Nobody handed me an outline. Nobody trampled on my feelings. Nobody shouted at me. Quite the contrary. *My* tantrums were tolerated.

When I impudently insisted that my novel, *Mountains of Gilead,* should have a "voice-over" plug at the end of the play, noting that the idea for the play came from the novel, Albert McCleery reluctantly gave in and let me have my way. He knew the plug would not help the novel, and he could not see any reason for it, but because I was the playwright he let me have my way. He humored me.

Many other producers, lesser men than Albert McCleery, would have fired me on the spot. Instead, when he found out that I had come to New York from Tennessee at my own expense and that I was nearly broke, he saw to it that I was put on the CBS payroll, so as to earn my expenses and a little more besides. On top of that, I was paid for my play—handsomely paid—and before the year was out Albert McCleery ran the play again, and I was paid again. This is the sort of stuff Albert McCleery is made of, and when I write another play for television (when and if) it will hopefully be for him.

The truth is that writers for television are probably kicked around more than any other group of people in any other profession in which people earn so much. Part of the reason the pay is so good is, I believe, to requite these writers for the punishment they must so often endure.

Albert McCleery does not kick writers around, and sponsors do not kick him around. The industry has no more success at this than the Germans had at it in World War II when this adventurous man dropped with his Airborne troops behind enemy lines.

The CBS Television Workshop operated behind enemy lines at the network, as it were. Shunted to an hour when most Americans were either in church or just waking up, we operated nevertheless, without the hounding of sponsors, and we knew victory. We knew the sweet success that only guerilla fighters can know, as when the critics began to set aside time on Sunday mornings to see what the CBS Television Workshop would have to say.

Donald Davidson had discussed a stage version of the play with me before my departure for Norway as a Fulbright Scholar in 1961, but it was not until I had been in Norway several months that the actual writing began. By then I had absorbed the saga tales of Iceland, in which nothing figures more positively than an overweening hunger for blood vengeance. The mood of these sagas fitted the feud-society atmosphere of the Southern hills exactly, it seemed to me.

Mr. Davidson's advice—well taken, I believe—was that the play should be expanded *from within*. The stage play could better document the doom of the Hedgepaths. It could carry the action beyond that of the television script.

Osborne Robinson, who designed the stage set for the Vanderbilt production of the play, was "on loan" to the Vanderbilt University Theater for the 1962–1963 session from the Northampton Repertory Theater, in England. In place of a commonplace tobacco-stained hillbilly jail, the Englishman designed a stunningly effective impressionistic version of a medieval British gaol, broodingly Anglo-Saxon. Behind Mr. Robinson's set, a cyclorama, blue with clouds in the early scenes,

ix

changed slowly to a bloody red for the final rendition by the banjo player. His lighting effects were just as imaginative.

The assumption is that, for a stage production, a unit set such as Osborne Robinson designed will be used, but any stage architect will see immediately that better advantage could be taken here with a revolving stage.

Joseph Wright's direction of the Vanderbilt production could not be faulted, and the actors, all of them students and amateurs, caught the spirit and performed magnificently. After the run at Vanderbilt, they took it to Humboldt, Tennessee, for a Saturday-evening performance in the Humboldt High School auditorium, where they played to a packed house.

The Conversion of Buster Drumwright has its beginnings in the influence and encouragement of many people. Had Edward Weeks, editor of the *Atlantic Monthly,* and Peter Davidson, director of the Atlantic Monthly Press, not begun writing to me in 1956 to encourage me to hang on, as they did, I would surely never have this play. Indeed, it was a short story which the *Atlantic* had rejected some fourteen times before they finally bought and published it, in 1959, which brought me to the attention of William Inge, the playwright, who, on the strength of the feeling displayed in this story, introduced me to Miss Audrey Wood, who in turn signed me to a contract with Music Corporation of America.

But lest you get the idea that I reached William

x

Inge by the story alone, let me add that Robert Bird, the Director of the Lincoln Foundation, and one of my most devoted champions, sent the short story to Mr. Inge, who happened to be a friend of his. (The story was "A Strange Sky," which appeared in the April 1959 issue of the *Atlantic*.)

A contract with MCA does not tell the whole story either. Before I could write a play, I needed a great deal of know-how, and this came from another friend, Edward Barry Roberts, and from his excellent book, *Television Writing and Selling* (Boston: The Writer, Inc., 1957).

Then there was Miss Wood's assistant, Aviva Hellman, who called me to come to New York when Albert McCleery called her and asked about new writers for television.

The idea for this book first occurred to me when Catherine Blankenship, East Coast story editor for CBS Television, mentioned to me that she was using *The Conversion of Buster Drumwright* with her classes at the Yale Drama School.

That there might be the possibility of a stage play from the television script came to me as a suggestion from my cousin, Stanley Musgrove, in Hollywood, and from Stan's friend, George Englund, at Universal-International Pictures.

There was William Zavis, who spent long evenings with me in Oslo, talking out the stage version. I will always be grateful to Bill for taking early drafts of the stage script around to his Norwegian theater friends to see what they thought of it and for encouraging me to send the final draft on to Joseph Wright at Vanderbilt University Theater.

Of all those who have believed in this play, no one has backed it more steadfastly than my agent, Jack Phelps.

It is my steadfast hope that this book will be of help and encouragement to anyone interested in writing for the theater. Television is no less the theater than the stage. A good play is a good play in either medium, and perhaps, in the end, that is what this book has to say.

JESSE HILL FORD

Humboldt, Tennessee
June 1964

Contents

Illustrations

Foreword

IN ONE of the best of his many notable essays on the art of the theater, the late Stark Young wrote with telling emphasis and wisdom about "purity in art." By "purity" he meant, of course, the quality of art as art—the art that is not propaganda, not egoistic self-expression, not the vain attempt of "naturalism" to imitate science or history, but the art that is true to itself and faithful to its subject no less than to its medium.

All purity in art begins with the translation of the essential idea [said Stark Young]. A work of art is pure in so far as it compels the ideas within it to stick to its own terms; it is pure in so far as the ideas within it find expression solely in these terms, without relying on anything else. In a work of art that is pure the idea—and every manifestation of it—discovers a body that is free of all characteristics not those of the art employed. . . . And that purity which we discern in the great artists' natures . . . and in great saints, arises from this; what they dream and desire is for its own end and perfection, free of considerations outside itself and untouched by the intrusions of another world of aims.*

Jesse Hill Ford's drama, *The Conversion of Buster Drumwright,* gives us a remarkable example of the operation of this high principle, so generally neglected

* "Seeing the Point," in *The Flower in Drama, and Glamour,* Charles Scribner's Sons, 1955, pp. 133–134.

in our confused period of tendentiousness, dull absurdity, and prurient sensationalism.

No outside consideration, no "intrusion of another world of aims" clouds the dramatic issues of this powerful play. As Hamlet's bounden duty was "to kill the King," so it is Ocie Hedgepath's bounden duty, as a Hedgepath, to revenge the murder of his sister and her infant. But the murderer, Buster Drumwright, is securely locked up in the county jail. Already he has been tried and condemned to hang. In three days more he most certainly *will* hang—unless the aroused community mobs the jail and lynches him first, as they are threatening to do when Ocie arrives on the scene. He has been away in Texas for many years, and as he passes through the crowd no one recognizes him as one of the Hedgepath boys. At home his frustrated brothers, Dan and Rance, egg Ocie on to find some way to get at Buster and execute the blood-vengeance that their code demands. Before the mob acts, cannot Ocie somehow reach through the cell bars and knife Buster, or strangle him? But how can Ocie argue or force his way past the Law—that is, past Deputy Sheriff Fate Stanhope, a well-armed and unyielding barrier? A preacher could get past the deputy —only a preacher—for neither the Law nor the mob would deny Buster a chance to repent and save his immortal soul. Will Ocie then pose as a preacher? He will. He does. He borrows a Bible from Dan's wife, Mary, the gentle Christian soul who is against all killing, and begins to read and remember. Especially does Ocie read the epistles of St. Paul and note a passage emphasized by Mary. Out of Ocie's impersonation come the series of quick-running scenes that lead to his interviews (at first violent and fruitless) with the condemned murderer and so finally to the triumphant climax during which, with the deputy's, the community's, and Buster's own consent, a bathtub is brought to the jail and filled with water for the baptism. Buster has been converted. But, in the astounding yet fully justified *peripateia,* Ocie has also converted himself. At the moment when with strong hands he douses Buster under water and holds him there, Ocie's "I baptize thee . . ." is saved from being blasphemy. He cannot drown Buster. He confesses—as Buster has confessed and repented.

Nothing could be more commendable in a dramatist than the perfect clarity and economy—and yes, in Stark Young's terms, the purity—with which Jesse Ford's play, especially the television play, moves toward its critical event. Nothing could be more absorbing, more possessing, to the fortunate audiences of the play, who are sure to be deeply moved, even brought to tears, in the exact proportion as they still belong to the ancient Christian society of the West—that society in which Christianity flowered out of a Judaic-Hellenistic soil.

Here we have no extraneous concerns. True, we have a preacher of the so-called "fundamentalist" type, with his Bible; but this is not the "Bible Belt" of hostile or servile caricature. We have a "mob" bent on lynching, true; but it is of the generic not the special journalistic or political sort. For even though the "mob" is in a sense unmistakably "Southern," as the militia muster of Justice Shallow in *Henry IV* is unmistakably "Warwickshire" or "Stratfordian," there is nothing in the play to interest any Mr. Fix-it. The people of the play are rural and Southern of the small-town and county-seat society, but we are not distracted by localisms of language or invited to condescend to picturesqueness or vulgarity. The scene (in the stage play at least) is East Tennessee, but the "regional" qualities of that interesting countryside figure here no more than the "regional" qualities of the plain of Thebes in Greek drama of the fifth century, B.C.

To compose with this kind of success, as Jesse Ford has done, in drama, story, or play, a writer must be "inside" the tradition that he explores, possessed by it while possessing it—inside as a Greek of Sophocles' time could be and as the best Irish dramatists (and few others) have been during the last half-century. As conscious artist the writer must also be "outside" his tradition in the design that he gives his material—that is, in his choice and use of the techniques available to him. To do otherwise would be to depend on naiveté and therefore on mere accident for success. Looking back to the nineteen-twenties, we can readily see that the now visible weakness and sterility of our American drama surely did not arise from its naiveté. The Eugene

O'Neills and their successors have not only the "out-
sideness" of the craftsman, which is their great, and
maybe their fatal, technical facility; but most unfor-
tunately they are outside of any tradition that can im-
part life and conviction to their works. They are "inside" of nothing but the theater—the now dying or
dead Broadway theater. All else they have repudiated
or lost, in order to offer commercial entertainment that
becomes ever more morose, depraved, or just silly.
Thomas Wolfe's satirical portrayal of George Pierce
Baker's famous 47 Workshop course at Harvard (in
Of Time and the River) touches, however blundering-
ly, upon an academic phase of the general malady. Too
many of Baker's aspirants, one fears, may have wanted
from him only "dramatic technique" to add to their
emptiness. But how could Baker, that excellent man,
make genuine dramatic artists out of hollow men?

The writer who is "inside" his tradition is no hollow
man. He has knowledge and belief that are not merely
his but are of his society. The voices of the past and of
the present that rests on that past ring through his
voice. Without such knowledge and belief there could
never be the conviction that informs the central con-
ception and spoken lines of Mr. Ford's play. There
would never be the sureness of touch that we find at
the critical points.

Take for illustration the passage where Ocie—already affected, though he hardly as yet realizes it, by
Mary's reading of a passage from Paul's Epistle to the

Colossians—must get Buster's consent to baptism. Ocie says, "You are going to be baptized, ain't you, Buster?" Then the dialogue proceeds:

BUSTER

You was going to tell me what happened to Paul, remember? After that I'll tell you if I am or if I ain't.

OCIE

That's fair and square.

BUSTER

How did he die, Preacher?

OCIE

Well, they trumped up this charge against him in Rome.

BUSTER

He was framed!

(*Ocie nods.*)

The dirty sapsuckers.

OCIE

So they handed down a verdict which was to throw him to the tigers and lions.

BUSTER

And did he take it all right?

OCIE

He never batted an eyelash. When they come and got him out of his cell, they didn't have to drag him.

BUSTER

He walked by his own self, didn't he? I knew he'd have acted that way.

OCIE

He had done been baptized, of course, and he knew there wasn't nothing to fear. He believed in Christ, and he knew where he was going.

BUSTER

And then what?

OCIE

So they got him to the edge of the pit where they kept these big hungry cats, and they was getting ready to push him, and he says, "Hold on. There won't hardly be any need for that." He wouldn't let them push him. . . . He looked them tigers and lions right in the eye. They was roaring and snarling. And then . . . he jumped.

BUSTER

I knew it. . . . He went under his own steam without nobody pushing and shoving at him.

The cold historian may say that St. Paul, being a Roman citizen, died by the executioner's sword, as he was entitled to die. He may also report that "second-century tradition" marks the spot of Paul's death as on the Ostian way, some three miles from Rome. Tradition of a richer and higher kind, working upon Ocie, transforms the make-believe preacher into a true one, whose *exemplum* is the generalized legend of the Christian martyr. That Paul was not "thrown" to the wild beasts but willingly "jumped" is Ocie's inspired emendation. Belief that has deep roots in Christian tradition as in his society now possesses Ocie as it also possesses the condemned man whom he has converted. Ocie is Paul's avatar. Buster has faith in Paul and in Ocie. The Law, in the person of Deputy Fate Stanhope, has accepted Ocie in somewhat the same way. So have the mob, members of which now drop all thought of lynching and bring buckets of water to fill the baptismal tub. And now the persuader is persuaded, the converter is converted as by a revelation. Ocie, who in

xxi

principle had been a kind of Saul, becomes himself a kind of Paul—a saver of souls rather than a blood-feud avenger.

Should Ocie then not suffer also the martyrdom of a Paul? The television play does not follow out this implication. After Buster and Ocie in turn have made their confessions to each other, Buster anxiously asks: "You . . . you still going to be there tomorrow, Preacher?" ("There" of course is the scaffold, to which Ocie has promised to walk with Buster.) Ocie answers, "I'll be there." The rest—as Ocie silently picks up his Bible—is wholly pictorial.

The full-length stage play, not confined to the stripped terseness of the television script—and in fact a little faultily diffuse at some points—carries through the latent sacrificial implication and thus well illustrates one commanding advantage of the stage over television. After baptism, when Buster is again locked in his cell, Ocie's two brothers, followed by Mary, rush through the mob, and Dan in vengeful madness cuts down Ocie with his knife. As he dies, Ocie says:

I had him . . . had him all the way under, like we planned. The power was pouring through my arms, all the power and vengeance—but, but it was . . . my arms shorted out on me. It come . . . him in yonder, *he* believed, and me . . . so did I believe too. I believed. The same as him, the same as Paul.

Seldom in these times does a playwright, story writer, or novelist open a vista that reaches as far as this. Our contemporary Jacobs may sometimes rest their heads on stones, realistic or even, in a warped and tedious way, symbolic. But they do not have visions that join heaven and earth. Their connections are with libraries, publishers, agents, and cocktail-party-givers, rather than with the people of a living society, and certainly are not celestial. But the Hedgepaths, Drumwrights, Stanhopes of Jesse Ford's play belong to Christendom—to the Christendom we recognize as American, as Southern, as honestly our own. What wonder that *The Conversion of Buster Drumwright,* from the beginning of its showing as a production of the Columbia Television Workshop, drowned some modern eyes unused to flow! It draws from the deepest fountains of race memory —from the veritable *anima mundi* about which Yeats was so much concerned. Yet the play is not exactly tragedy, though it is near that level. Perhaps we should think of it as high comedy, which can be as serious and moving as tragedy. At any rate it seems proper to add here that the qualities that give the play its excellence also appear in Jesse Ford's wide-ranging stories, from his initial success with "The Surest Thing in the Show Business" on to such later pieces as "How the Mountains Are" and the beautifuly written "Look Down, Look Down." These may not be quite as central to our deepest concerns as *The Conversion of Buster Drumwright,* but surely they betoken much strong work to come. The play, however, which we have here in its two forms, illustrating by unusual good fortune the problems of composition in two media, is something more than just a foretaste. It is accomplishment, made available in this volume for study and contemplation. Yet here it is only literature if it is only read; it will be truly and fully itself only when seen and heard, on screen and stage, as we have every right to hope it often will be.

DONALD DAVIDSON

The Television Script

Characters

Scenes

ACT ONE

ACT TWO

ACT THREE

Act One

[FADE IN: The exterior of the Trammel, Tennessee, county jail at night]

(*Seated on the front steps of the jail is Fate Stanhope, a double-barreled shotgun resting across his knees. The sounds of a small but angry mob some of whom hold torches that flare in the foreground, add to a general atmosphere of uneasiness. Above, and to the right, behind Stanhope, Buster Drumwright grips the bars of the jail window and glares out at the crowd. As we draw back, we see Ocie on the apparent front edge of the crowd. The Bystander does not see Ocie at first.*)

BYSTANDER

Turn him over to us. Give us the prisoner, Fate!

(*He holds up a battered rectangular gallon can. His other fist shakes a coil of thin rope.*)

Danged murderer!

(*Looking upward*)

We mean to burn you, Drumwright!

OCIE

So that's Buster Drumwright.

BYSTANDER (*Seeing Ocie for the first time*)

That's him, all right. And we aim to put the gasoline to him.

7

OCIE

You mean lynch him?

BYSTANDER

That's what this rope's for.

(*Yelling*)

How about it, Fate? Do you give him to us, or do we come after him?

FATE

(*He raises the shotgun and fires it into the air.*) Get back now. Ain't nobody taking the prisoner from me. Fair and legal, that's how it's gonna be. You got three days to wait until the hanging.

BUSTER

Come get me, Fat Boy! Just try it!

FATE

I mean it, get back now!

(*Looking up*)

Hush, Drumwright!

OCIE

So that's him.

BYSTANDER

Oh, it's lots and lots of folks come just to get a look at him. I guess he's about the meanest killer Tennessee ever had!

(*With pride*)

And there he rests, in our jail. Including women and children, he killed *seventeen people,* Drumwright did . . .

(*The Bystander has warmed up and is preparing to*

8

bend Ocie's ear properly about Buster Drumwright.
He is talking out of the side of his mouth, keeping an
eye on Fate Stanhope. When he looks around, Ocie
is already leaving. Puzzled for an instant, the Bystander
stares after Ocie. Then he turns and begins shaking
the rope and yelling, as though reminded of why he
is there.)
All right, Deputy! Give us Buster Drumwright. We
mean business!

SCENE TWO

[DISSOLVE TO: The interior of the Hedgepath cabin]
(*The Preacher is talking earnestly to Dan, Rance, and*
Mary.)

PREACHER

The whole town feels like you do. But we can't have
the stain of a lynching on our hands. We profess to be
Christians, after all. That's why I went to see Buster
Drumwright today.

DAN

You mean you went inside the jail and saw him,
Preacher?

PREACHER

It was my duty to see if I could help prepare him to
meet God. I saw him, but it wasn't any use. Drumwright cursed me and laughed at me.

9

RANCE

That's just like him. Anybody that would kill a woman and her baby!

PREACHER

Just let me leave this thought with you. Try to remember it. *God* will punish Buster Drumwright. Shall we have prayer?

(*They all kneel in a circle, joined by Mary.*)

O God of mercy, God of forgiveness, help us, we pray, to wipe all desire for vengeance from our hearts, and O Lord, help our little community in this time of crisis! Bring us to salvation in the end. We pray in the name of Jesus Christ. Amen.

(*Standing*)

Goodbye.

MARY

Thank you, Preacher. You got Dan to listen. I've been so afraid.

PREACHER

God is helping us. Have faith, Mary. Goodnight.

(*He leaves.*)

DAN

Is he gone?

RANCE

Shhh! Let him get gone aways.

MARY

Dan! You ain't *still* aiming to do it!

DAN

Hush, woman! Keep out of what ain't none of your affair!

10

MARY (*Pleading*)

But I'm your wife, ain't I?

DAN (*Raising his hand menacingly*)

I might have to slap you down less'n you hush!

OCIE (*Stepping out of the shadows into the room*)

No call to slap her. She'll keep her mouth shut.

RANCE

Ocie! We was just wondering when you'd be back from the jail. The preacher just now give us some song and dance about forgiving Buster Drumwright.

OCIE

I heard him. I was on the porch.

DAN

Well, how was it? Did you think up a plan?

OCIE

It was like you said. I got up so close that them two barrels on his shotgun looked like a pair of caves. (*Pausing*)

I couldn't hardly believe it was the same fellow, little Fate Stanhope. Why, Fate was just a little kid, maybe five years old, when I left from here. But there he was tonight, yonder on those jail steps with that shotgun. He looked big as a bear. It come to me then, how long I been away from Trammel.

RANCE

Did anybody recognize you, Ocie?

OCIE

Not a soul. I guess they've forgot there ever was anybody called Ocie Hedgepath. In fact, it weren't hardly any of them I recognized. A place changes.

11

(*Pausing*)

Like that old store where I used to get me a penny sack of licorice whenever Paw let us go to town with him —it's burnt up. The store's gone. It's a filling station on that corner now.

(*Pausing*)

I was thirteen years old when I left here. Just a little old kid, running away to look over the world.

DAN

You come back at a good time, Ocie. When your family needed you. It's us in this thing together now, ain't it, Ocie? It's the Hedgepath boys together from now on . . .

RANCE

Like when we was kids! When Kathleen was . . . was alive. I remember—she used to sit in that corner there, by the fire, mending. She mended our socks and shirts.

DAN

Recall what a pretty voice she had? Sometimes I dream I hear her singing. I wake up and I'm all warm feeling, for it seems like back long ago when Kathleen lived here with us. And then it comes to me what happened, and I start grieving and hurting inside . . .

OCIE

You never said just how it happened—how Buster Drumwright done it.

RANCE

It was too awful, Ocie. Kathleen was living alone with her baby, too proud to come back to us after her husband left her. Drumwright got her to fix him a meal

12

somehow. Maybe she took pity on him. The plates was still on the table when I got there. He had took a knife and . . .

(*Pausing*)

. . . and her and her baby boy was laying there.

(*The horror comes back to him. It enters his face.*)

OCIE

So he done it with a knife. I heard it in Galveston, Texas, in this barbershop. This man read the newspaper out loud, how Drumwright was caught and had confessed. I didn't get no haircut. I lit out then and come home. Only I never knew it was a knife.

(*The horror reaches Ocie.*)

DAN (*Explosively*)

Then how are we going to get him! Let me go. I'll walk up to that jail. I'll shoot him where he stands in the window.

RANCE

Wait! It ain't no sense in *that*. We got to one of us get our *hands* on him. You can't just shoot him quick like that. Buster Drumwright has got to suffer, to pay for what he done to Kathleen.

DAN

Well, then how *can* we get him? Ain't we been all over it a hundred times? Listen, that mob's gonna get him first if we don't hurry. We got just two more nights after tonight—just *two!*

OCIE

But you'll never get past Fate Stanhope's shotgun. It was plain from the first minute I saw him.

13

DAN

Naw, none of us could. And yet . . . the Preacher, he went down there.

(*Pausing*)

And they let him right in the jail. He said so here tonight.

RANCE

And then he come here to talk forgiveness. Praying! Do I feel like praying when the man that killed Kathleen is down there in that jail? I got to do something —now! I got to!

DAN

Then let's go! We'll shoot Fate Stanhope right off them steps if we have to. We'll . . .

OCIE

Hold on. It's no need of any more of us getting killed.

DAN (*Alarmed*)

Ocie, you ain't afraid? Don't you want this insult off our name?

OCIE

Listen a minute. Now that preacher, he got in to see Buster Drumwright because *he* was a preacher. A preacher could get him!

RANCE

Sure, a preacher. They can't refuse a preacher.

DAN (*Impatiently*)

But we ain't *got* a preacher.

RANCE

But we do, we have got one. Somebody they'd never suspect . . .

14

DAN

Ocie!

DAN (*Pausing*)

Will you try it, Ocie?

OCIE

I don't look much like a preacher. But . . .

(*Hesitantly*)

. . . if I could get into the jail I could . . .

DAN

You could get him! You can pretend like you're a preacher.

RANCE

All you need is a *Bible.*

MARY

This is wrong! Don't pretend to be a preacher, Ocie. It's blasphemy.

DAN (*Angrily*)

Get out your *Bible,* Mary. We need it for Ocie—for Brother Ocie.

(*He winks at the others.*)

Go on, bring that *Bible.* Hear me, woman?

MARY

(*Approaching slowly, clasping the book to her breast with both hands. She is fearful.*)

Don't do it, don't do it, Dan!

DAN

(*He wrests the book from her and pushes her roughly away.*)

Give it here! Here's our *Bible,* Brother Ocie—your *Bible.*

15

OCIE

(*He takes it. The book is strange to his hands.*)
They say you have to be called to preach. The Lord
calls you some way. That's what I always heard.

RANCE

You *look* like a preacher, Ocie. Don't he, Dan? It's
the book. It's how you hold it. Don't he, Dan? Don't he
sort of look like one?

DAN

I'll swear, I believe he does. It's going to work.
(*Jubilantly*)
By gum, it is!

RANCE

Not so fast.
(*Calmly*)
Ocie, listen. Don't get excited. You got to fool Fate
Stanhope, and he ain't going to be easy to deceive.

OCIE

Maybe I could carry a good knife and do Drumwright
like he done Kathleen!

DAN

Yeah. A good knife! Take mine.
(*Laying an ugly knife, unclapsed, on the table*)

RANCE

No knife. What if Fate searched you? What's a
preacher doing with a knife?
(*Pausing*)
All you need is your hands.
(*Ocie looks down at his hands, clasped about the
book.*)

16

Your hands. They'll go to his throat just like two trained hounds. They'll strangle him real slow. See?

OCIE

(*Pushing the knife away as he speaks*)

I see it now. I won't need no knife. I'll . . . I'll just think what he done to Kathleen and her baby boy. (*He is overcome, almost, by a feeling of wonderment.*) My hands will fasten theirselves on Buster Drumwright's throat and crush his life right out of him. (*Putting the Bible down on the table beside Dan's knife and looking at his trembling hands*) My hands will do it! (*Fiercely*) They will!

RANCE

Then go along. Time's getting away from us. Get him. Get him for us, Ocie!

OCIE

I'll get him. (*Taking up the Bible*) I'll get him! (*We see Mary's worried face.*)

SCENE THREE

[Dissolve to: The exterior of the jail] (*Ocie comes up to the jail porch steps, where Fate Stanhope sits. Fate throws up the shotgun, startled.*)

17

FATE

Hold it right there, fellow.

OCIE

I didn't mean to startle you.

FATE

You better watch how you sneak up on people! I aim to save Buster Drumwright for the gallows, Mister. I thought I had run the last one of you fellows away from here.

OCIE

I ain't a part of that bunch, Sheriff.

FATE

I ain't the sheriff. I'm only his nephew.

OCIE

Well, whatever you are, I ain't up to no mischief. (*Patronizingly*)
I know it must be rough, sitting out here at night, all alone, with nothing but the crickets and the moths to keep a fellow company.

FATE (*Patting the shotgun*)

This gun's company enough. Two nights more, and me and this gun can rest.

OCIE

Hanging's that soon? It don't leave me much time.

FATE (*Suspiciously, turning the gun slightly towards Ocie*)

Don't give you much time for *what*?

OCIE

To bring Buster Drumwright to Christ. You see, I come all the way from Texas. I . . . I felt the call to save him.

18

FATE

You say you come all the way from Texas? Well, you come a long way for nothing. Nobody can save Buster Drumwright.

OCIE

God could.

FATE

Well, I wouldn't say that *God* couldn't. I wouldn't go that far, of course. But do you know how many folks he's murdered? Do you, Preacher?

OCIE

I ain't heard tell the exact number, no.

FATE

He's killed *seventeen*—that's seventeen he *remembers* about. You can't save him, Preacher.

OCIE

But you got to let me try. I come all this long way.

FATE

Come back tomorrow. See my uncle about it. He's sheriff. I couldn't take the responsibility—not at night when I'm here all by myself. Why, Drumwright might get his hands on you through the bars! You come back tomorrow.

OCIE

Look, brother, I've done thought this all out. It wouldn't do me no good to come see him with the crowds out front. The gospel message needs to reach a man when it's quiet. And I don't have much time. You said so yourself, brother.

FATE

How in the world can I make you understand? Now

19

you're a preacher, and maybe Buster Drumwright is some sort of challenge to *you*, but he's a problem to me. I have to lock myself up in that jail just to take his supper tray to his cell. You don't know it, but the way the feeling is around here, I never know what I'll find when I get back down to these here steps. Why, I ain't even taken his grub to him *yet*. It's been so bad tonight I never had a chance.

OCIE

Give me the tray, brother. I'll take it to him. And while he eats, I can talk to him about his salvation. Now that's a fair offer, ain't it? Well, ain't it?

FATE (*Pausing, looking at Ocie before he decides, weighing the proposition*)

All right. But I'll have to lock you in, understand?

OCIE

I don't mind. I guess I'll need the key to his cell, won't I?

FATE

We don't unlock his cell, not for nobody. Just slip the tray under the cell door.

(*Standing, he takes the ring of jail keys off his belt and turns to the door.*)

OCIE

But how can I talk to him without unlocking his cell and going in to see him?

FATE

Talk through the bars. It's safer. Now you'll be extra careful, won't you?

20

OCIE (*Deciding not to press the issue concerning the cell key*)

I'll be extra careful.

(*Fate picks up the cloth-covered tray of food and hands it to Ocie, who stands behind him while the deputy unlocks the steel door. The door slams behind Ocie as he steps through it carrying the tray in one hand and the Bible in the other. We hear Ocie's footsteps echoing down the hallway, and we see Fate Stanhope's alert face as he sits back down on the porch steps.*)

SCENE FOUR

[DISSOLVE TO: Cell corridor]

(*Ocie is in the hallway outside Buster Drumwright's cell. The prisoner, who has been napping, wakes up, quick and catlike. He rubs his eyes. Then he approches the bars, looking out like a caged animal. For a moment, neither man speaks.*)

BUSTER

Who are you?

OCIE

I brought your supper.

BUSTER

About time. My belly's growling.

(*Ocie stoops and shoves the tray under the door. Buster*)

*snatches up the tray quickly and backs up to the steel
bench in his cell, where he sits down and begins to
eat.*)

Cold supper every night. Covered with cold grease . . .
(*He is suddenly suspicious.*)

Who are you anyway?

OCIE

A preacher.

BUSTER (*Continuing to eat, nimbly*)

Well, get away from me then. I don't have no use for
preachers. One was in here today, trying to make me
say I was sorry for what I done. Why should I be
sorry? I got tomorrow, I got the next day, and
then . . .

OCIE

Just let me say something.

BUSTER

Who are you, anyway? Some windbag trying to make
a big show, trying to show folks how you converted
Buster Drumwright? Well, I already belong to the
devil. Yeah! And you can go to hell! So git!

(*Standing, Buster flings the tray at Ocie and rushes at
the bars. He comes close, but not quite close enough.
Ocie is tempted to try to reach for him, but he controls
the impulse. Then Buster, turning away, leaps to the
cell window and grabs the bars, looking down where
Fate Stanhope is sitting on the jail steps.*)

Get this preacher out of here! Hear me, Stanhope?

(*Ocie turns to go as Buster leaves the window and
stares after him.*)

22

BUSTER

Huh! Some preacher. Just hot air—that's all you are!
(*Laughing*)
Git!

SCENE FIVE

[DISSOLVE TO: The interior of the Hedgepath cabin]
(*Ocie enters. His brothers await him, tense with
anxiety.*)

DAN

Did you get him? Did you, Ocie? What happened?
(*Ocie pauses. For a moment, he cannot find the words
to tell them.*)

OCIE

I got inside the jail.

DAN

And you got him! You just had to get him. Your
hands, they . . .
(*Angrily*)
You didn't get him! Why? What's got into you?

RANCE

Hush, Dan. Let Ocie talk!

DAN

You didn't go yellow, did you, Ocie?

OCIE

Nobody went yellow! I couldn't get my hands on him.
Stanhope let me in the jail, but he won't let me in

23

Buster's cell. There wasn't no chance to grab him through the bars.

RANCE

And Stanhope believed you was a preacher.

OCIE

Yep. And he's going to let me in the jail tomorrow night, *again*. Now when I take Buster his supper tray, when he squats down to get the tray, I'll reach through the bars and grab him. I'll beat his brains out on the bars.

RANCE

But can't you get the key to his cell? You might miss him grabbing that way through the bars.

DAN

He's right, Ocie. We don't want to take no chances on you missing Buster Drumwright. You're our last chance.

OCIE

I asked Stanhope about getting into the cell. I asked him first thing. But he said nothing doing. And I didn't get nowhere trying to convert Buster. He cursed me before I could get started.

DAN

I see the trouble now. You're really trying to *preach* to him.

OCIE

Well, I got to get him close up to those bars some way. How else would a preacher act if he didn't try to preach to him?

24

(*Ocie flips through the Bible in his hands.*)
He has to believe I'm a preacher.

RANCE

Ocie's right, Dan. It's a better chance he can lay his hands on him if he tries to convert him than if he tries that grabbing business over the supper tray. If that first grab missed, the show would be over. Then Buster would know what was *really* up, and we'd never get him.

DAN (*Sullenly*)

Maybe. But if it don't work, we can still go down there, the three Hedgepath brothers, and shotgun or no shotgun, one of us can get through to Buster Drumwright. (*Pausing*)
Well, I'm turning in.

RANCE

Me too.

(*Ocie remains seated at the table, turning the pages in the Bible.*)
Ain't you going to bed, Ocie?

OCIE

I got to study this *Bible*. I got to figure how I'm going to preach to him.

(*As the brothers laugh at this and leave, Mary comes to the table. Her hair is down and she is in her night dress.*)

MARY

I'm glad you didn't do it, Ocie. I keep hoping you'll give this idea up. It's blasphemy.

25

DAN (*Not seen*)

Get here, gal! Get to bed.

MARY (*Loudly*)

I'm coming!

(*Softly*)

I'm glad you didn't, Ocie. I prayed.

OCIE

Get away! Go to bed and leave me be. I've got to think and study.

MARY (*Softly*)

Goodnight, Ocie.

DAN

Mary! Ain't I told you once to come to bed!

(*Ocie looks up as she quickly leaves, but he says nothing. He turns his attention back to the Bible, forming the words he reads, slowly, his lips moving, but making no sound.*)

SCENE SIX

[DISSOLVE TO: The exterior of the jail]

(*The Bystander stands in front of the jail, watching curiously as Ocie approaches. We hear noises from the crowd.*)

BYSTANDER (*Loudly*)

Well, look what we got here! Yonder comes the preacher.

26

(*With hearty sarcasm*)

Studying that Bible mighty hard, ain't you, Preacher, eh? That's a preacher for you, all the time a-studying . . .

OCIE

Everybody needs to study this book. The whole world needs to read it.

BYSTANDER

You must be the one that's trying to convert Buster Drumwright, eh?

(*Ocie nods.*)

Well, you'll never bring that heathen murderer to Christ.

(*Pausing*)

Say, ain't I seen you before, Preacher?

OCIE

Maybe. I was here last night.

BYSTANDER (*Pausing, then suddenly remembering*)

So you was! But I never suspected you for a preacher. Hey, Deputy, here's your preacher back.

FATE

Okay, Preacher. Come on. The rest of you folks stand back!

(*Buster appears at the cell window above.*)

BUSTER

You back, Preacher? I thought I ran you off for good.

BYSTANDER

You hush hollering that way at a man of God!

BUSTER

What do you care, you old tub of guts?

27

BYSTANDER

You better watch it, Drumwright. The citizens of this county have had just about enough of your wicked tongue!

CROWD

Let's get him! What are we waiting for?

FATE (*Firmly*)

We're hanging him fair and legal, day after tomorrow.

BYSTANDER (*Derisively*)

Fair and legal. Ha! How fair and legal was he when he stabbed the Hedgepath gal and her baby? Huh?

FATE

Now folks, go home! Come on, Preacher.

(*Ocie is standing with the supper tray in his hand. The deputy lets him in the jail and locks the door after him. Buster is still at the window above, smiling down at the crowd.*)

BUSTER (*Shouting as the crowd leaves*)

That's the way! Go on home!

FATE (*From below, not seen*)

Shut up, Buster!

SCENE SEVEN

[DISSOLVE TO: Cell corridor]

(*Ocie's footsteps approach down the hall. From the window, Buster turns to see Ocie standing outside his cell.*)

28

OCIE

Here's your supper. This time it's hot.
(*He stoops down and pushes the tray part way beneath the door.*)

BUSTER

Push it all the way—all the way under, Preacher.
(*Ocie pushes the tray well under the door and stands back.*)
That's it.
(*Buster takes the tray to his bench and begins to eat. He looks at Ocie musingly.*)
So you really come back. I never seen such grit in a preacher before.

OCIE

I have something to tell you. I got good news for you.

BUSTER

For me? Good news? You ought to be in the vaudeville, cracking jokes like that.

OCIE

Just because you're in jail, that's no reason to give up hope.

BUSTER

Who says I've give up hope? Huh? I'm going to bust out of this tin can!

OCIE

Well, what if you don't bust out, though. What then?

BUSTER

They'll just hang me, that's all. What do you *think* they'll do?
(*A pause*)

29

OCIE

But after you're dead, where will you go then?

BUSTER

You're like the rest of them sapsucking preachers, ain't you? Always talking about hell. Well, I'm going there. So save your sapsucking wind.

(*Pausing*)

Hell, that's all you know to tell a fellow about. And you say you've got good news!

OCIE

Did you ever hear of St. Paul?

BUSTER

Paul? Ain't he in the *Bible*? I heard of him, sure. It's people named after him walking around today.

(*Pausing*)

In fact, I had a friend once named Paul. He was running off some moonshine whiskey at our still, and this revenue agent shot him right through the head. I looked down beside me, and Paul was dead, and his eyes was even still open, just like yours. I grabbed my rifle, and I rolled sideways about fifty steps before I started shooting. I killed three of them sapsuckers, and the fourth one, he run off before I could get a bead on him. Let me tell you, Preacher, he caught air! And then . . . then, after it was over, I went back to where Paul was laying, and . . . it wasn't Paul anymore. It was something else, like I never saw before, until then.

(*Pausing*)

What was you saying?

30

OCIE

I was saying about Paul. He was in jail plenty of times. They got him on vagrancy and throwed him in the tank. They beat him up and made him sleep with the drunks.

BUSTER

Don't kid me. Don't try to pull my leg, Preacher. Nobody in the *Bible* was ever in jail—not Paul, anyway. Not a good guy like him.

OCIE

No, it's true, sure enough. Paul hoboed and bummed around. He didn't do nothing *bad,* you know. But they still got him every so often on vagrancy. Why, once they had him in prison at this town, and the Lord sent an earthquake. It broke open the cell doors, and Paul and his buddies just walked out, big as you please. He even had the Mayor and the Board of Aldermen come up and apologize for their being locked up in the first place. It's the kind of man Paul was. *He* never give up hope. No sir!

BUSTER (*Less incredulous*)

I . . . I don't believe there could be nothing like that in the *Bible.*

OCIE (*Holding up the Bible*)

Listen, friend. I just got through reading it *last night.*

BUSTER

There you go. Preaching again! Trying to trick me with that stuff about Paul. Paul wouldn't use no tricks. He wouldn't have to!

31

OCIE

Well, Paul was a preacher. He preached the good news.

BUSTER (*Almost reverently*)

I never thought of that—that Paul was a preacher. (*Pausing*)

A good guy like him. What would I have to do to be saved, Preacher? Not that I'd *do* it—don't get me wrong.

OCIE

Oh, it's easy. Just repent of your sins, is all. Then you confess Christ as your Saviour, and you're baptized.

BUSTER

Baptized?

OCIE

It's where they put you under the water and wash all your . . .

BUSTER

Sure, I know what it is. I heard of being baptized before. But I never was, of course.

(*With quick anger*)

And I never will be. How could you baptize anybody through this?

(*Grabbing the cell door, rattling it*)

What a joke!

(*Buster laughs bitterly.*)

OCIE

If you was really interested in getting baptized I could ask.

BUSTER (*Bitterly*)

Forget it, Preacher. It was a crazy idea.

(*Pausing*)

32

What ever happened to him, anyway?

OCIE

(*He is distracted, for he is preoccupied with an idea.*)
What happened? To who?

BUSTER

To Paul? What ever become of him?

OCIE

Oh, why he went on preaching.
(*Vaguely*)
They even converted this jailer once and . . .

BUSTER

I'm talking about the end. How did Paul die? What
happened to him?

OCIE

(*His face is a blank, for he has been trapped at a bad
moment. He doesn't know the answer, so he stalls.*)
What makes you so interested in that, all of a sudden?
Ain't . . . ain't how he *lived* more important?

BUSTER (*After a pause*)
Not to me, it ain't.

OCIE (*Astonished*)
Well, look, I got to be leaving.

BUSTER (*Sardonically*)
I might have knew you would! You ain't coming back,
either, are you, Preacher? Well, you may as well give
up, because nobody is converting Buster Drumwright.
See what I mean?

OCIE

Look, I got to go. But I promise to come back tomorrow
night. I'll tell you what happened to him, to Paul, tomorrow, all right?

33

BUSTER

Why not now? Any preacher would know that, wouldn't he? Don't you know?

OCIE (*Angrily*)

Sure I do! But it's a long story. You can't tell it in two words—not about somebody as important as Paul. And anyway, you ain't interested in getting baptized.

BUSTER

I never said I wasn't *interested,* did I?

(*Ocie has turned to leave. Now he comes back.*)

OCIE

If something could be figured out—if it could be fixed some way—would you be baptized?

BUSTER

I . . . well, I don't know.

OCIE

Look, you ain't got much time! There's only tomorrow night, and then . . .

BUSTER

The rope. I know it.

OCIE

Well, how about it?

BUSTER

See you tomorrow night then, Preacher?

OCIE

Yeah.

(*Ocie's expression shows his relief, and then his puzzlement, as he realizes that his plan is succeeding.*)

SCENE EIGHT

[DISSOLVE TO: The exterior of the jail]

(*Fate Stanhope is sitting in a chair on the porch. On hearing Ocie's footsteps coming down the hall, Fate gets up and unlocks the door.*)

FATE (*As Ocie comes out*)

No luck again, huh, Preacher? Like I already said, there ain't any chance of converting him.

OCIE

I wouldn't exactly say it wasn't no *chance.*

FATE (*Incredulous, but unwilling to dispute a man of God*)

You ain't kidding me, Preacher?

OCIE

He's *a-teetering* on the very *edge.* I think he'll call on the name of Jesus Christ tomorrow. I seen it happen too many times not to know. Only one thing . . .

FATE

You ought to know. But still, he . . .

(*Becoming more sure he has the reason now*)

. . . he might be fooling you.

OCIE (*Firmly*)

He ain't fooling. Only thing is . . .

FATE (*Humbled now before the reality of the conversion*)

What's bothering you?

OCIE

Like he said just now. Even if he does get converted, it wouldn't be no way for me to baptize him through them bars. It kind of hurts me to think on it.

35

FATE

Ain't it no way else except you have to baptize him?

OCIE

If he ain't baptized, he ain't saved. If he did . . .
(*Pausing*)
. . . say he did take Christ. You think we could take him out to baptize him?

FATE (*Hesitantly*)

If it was anything else but to baptize him . . .

OCIE

You can't hardly tell him "no" to that, can you?

FATE

Well, maybe if you got a tub, we could put it up in the hall outside the cell. But naw—naw, I couldn't take on that responsibility. I . . .

OCIE

You better think a minute.

FATE (*Giving in now; deciding firmly*)

You're right, Preacher. I couldn't stand in the way of no man's salvation and live with myself after that. You get a tub.

OCIE

I'll be back here tomorrow night.
(*Leaving, turning away to hide his elation*)

FATE (*Seen over Ocie's shoulder*)

Just bring the tub. It'll be all right.
(*Ocie leaves as we hold on Fate, close in, watching Ocie go.*)
[THE END OF ACT ONE]

36

Act Two

SCENE ONE

[DISSOLVE TO: The interior of the Hedgepath cabin]
(*Dan's knife peels a sliver off the piece of wood he is whittling. Then, suddenly he stabs the knife down into the bench he is sitting on. It is the same night.*)

DAN

I'm sick and tired of waiting, of wondering every minute, has he done it or not.

RANCE

Don't fly off the handle.

MARY

Your conscience is bothering you, Dan.

DAN

You shut up!
(*We hear Ocie's footsteps on the porch. He is running as he enters, his face flushed, his eyes wild.*)

RANCE

Ocie!

OCIE

I've run nearly all the way.

DAN

You got him, didn't you?

MARY (*Fearfully*)

No!

DAN

(*He stands, grabbing Mary by the shoulders and shaking her fiercely.*)

Ain't I told you to keep your mouth out of this?

OCIE

Leave her be! Leave her alone and listen.

(*Dan flings her aside and turns to Ocie. About to speak, he is interrupted by Rance.*)

RANCE

You got him, did you?

OCIE

No, I ain't got him. But I found the *way* to get him. I tell you, it might just work.

RANCE

Did you hear that, Dan? It's going to work!

DAN (*Dejectedly*)

When you come in, so fast and all, I thought you had done got him. I thought . . .

OCIE

It's all nearly fixed up. It hit me all of a sudden tonight when Buster asked about baptism.

MARY

Baptism? You mean you're really converting him, Ocie?

DAN (*Angrily*)

No, he ain't converting him. For the last time, Ocie's trying to kill him. He's *going to* kill him.

RANCE

Go on. What happened?

38

OCIE

It come to me that, if I could get my hands on him to baptize him, then I could . . .

RANCE

You could strangle him, like we planned.

OCIE

Better than that. I could push him down under the water, down all the way under, and just hold him there.

DAN

You're going to do it! I knowed all along you could. You're going to get him.

OCIE

So when I come out, I asked the deputy, how about it, could I baptize him. Derned if he didn't say I could!

DAN

I knowed it! I been praying you'd get him, Ocie.

OCIE

Only there's just this one hitch.

RANCE

A hitch?

OCIE

Yeah. Buster ain't said for certain if he will be baptized or not.

DAN

But you just said he would.

OCIE

I said he was interested. I need . . . I need to know some Bible stuff. I need . . .

DAN

Get over here, Mary, and listen here to what Ocie needs.

OCIE

I need to know what ever become of Paul, that's what I need first—how he died.

DAN

How did Paul die? Tell him, Mary.

MARY

(*She is without hope now, her spirit broken.*)
He was martyred. The *Bible* don't say, but they think he was killed at Rome.

OCIE

But how did they kill him?

DAN

Tell him!

MARY

I imagine the lions tore him apart. I guess . . . I don't know. They used to throw them to the lions . . .

OCIE

That's good enough. I'll improve on that some. Buster ought to go for that.

DAN

He will, he'll go for it like a chicken on a June bug!

RANCE

What else do you need to know?

OCIE

Well, I need some scripture to read to him, something to melt his heart like, something maybe to make him feel like crying.

40

DAN (*Taking up the Bible from the table and handing it to Mary*)

All right, woman, you hear him. Find him some scripture like that! You always got your nose in this book.

MARY

I . . .

DAN

Find it, I said! I'll give you about one minute flat.
(*Mary takes the Bible in her trembling hands. She is almost in tears.*)

MARY

I like the third chapter of Colossians.

OCIE

Did Paul write it?

MARY

Yes.

DAN

All right, let's hear it.

MARY

(*She finds the place and begins to read.*)

"If ye then be risen with Christ, seek those things which are above, where Christ sitteth on the right hand of God. Set your affection on things above, not on things on the earth. For ye are dead, and your life is hid with Christ in God. When Christ, who is our life, shall appear, then shall ye also appear with him in glory."

DAN

That's enough.

RANCE

What do you think, Ocie?

41

OCIE

He's so near to death it ought to get him.

DAN

It will, it'll get him. He'll bawl like a baby. Mark the place, Mary.

OCIE (*Taking the open Bible from Mary*)
I'll mark it myself.
(*Reading*)
"When Christ, who is our life, shall appear, then shall ye also appear with him in glory." That's a mighty big order for Buster Drumwright, ain't it? Can you see *him* in glory?

RANCE

In hell, that's the only place I can see him. And you're going to send him there.

OCIE (*Winking*)
Not if he's baptized! I'm sending him to heaven, remember?

RANCE

It's like killing two birds with one stone. You save him and send him to heaven all in one smooth operation, just by holding him under the water a little longer. Well, you need anything else?

OCIE

I've got to get an old bathtub somewhere and get it hauled up to the jail. We'll set it up in the hall outside his cell.

DAN

And when you take him out, you'll be thinking about

42

Kathleen and her baby, and you'll have the steel in your hands to wipe this stain off the name of Hedgepath. You'll push him down under that water . . . and then, when you don't pull him out, he'll have time to think about the ones he killed, before his breath gives out. Before his breath gives out he'll know it's a revenger has him, and then he'll commence to suck water till all the wind is bubbled up out of him. I wish it was me doing it instead of you, Ocie!

OCIE

I'll be thinking about you, Dan.

RANCE

And me. Think of me, too.

OCIE

I will, Rance.

DAN

I dreamed last night you done it, Ocie. When it's done I won't fear so to dream about Kathleen and how it was, long ago. I can wake up then and know we avenged her death. I been fearing it would fail, I guess. But now . . .

OCIE

I won't fail. Once I get him in that tub I'll have him. Are you going to show me the place where Kathleen is buried with her baby?

DAN

After you've killed Buster, I'll take you there. It's a right pretty spot, all green and grassy and nice, and it's a redbud tree growing there. She liked to see the red-

43

buds so much, when they come out all flowering in the spring. I figured it was the right place for her to lay.

OCIE

I recall how she loved the springtime. I recall it now.

RANCE

And I recall how she pulled flowers and pinned them on her's and Maw's bonnets when they went to church. I tell you, Ocie, we nearly died when she left to get married. And now this—

OCIE

I need to get some sleep. I'll need my strength tomorrow evening.

(*He stands, holding the Bible.*)

MARY

Did you mark the place?

(*She draws him aside.*)

OCIE

Ain't this here the place? I've marked the place here.

MARY

(*She speaks swiftly, as the two other men, Dan and Rance, stretch and prepare to go off to bed. They do not hear her.*)

Would Kathleen want you to do this, Ocie? I knew her too, Ocie. I loved her too.

OCIE (*Turning away*)

Lay off! This ain't none of your business. You never loved her, to say such a thing!

MARY (*Pleading*)

I did. I did love her, Ocie.

44

(*But he walks away, apparently unmoved. Looking after him, her face cannot mask its terror and distress. Clasping her hands together, she lowers her face to them, as though in prayer.*)

SCENE TWO

[DISSOLVE TO: The interior of the Hedgepath cabin, the next night]

(*Ocie lies on a cot, his head pillowed on his arm. Fully clothed, he holds the Bible on his chest. The book is closed. Mary is with him in the room.*)

MARY

Are you asleep, Ocie?

OCIE (*Gruffly*)

No.

MARY

You been laying there all day. Ain't you hungry?

OCIE

I already told you, I ain't hungry. I'll have plenty of time for eating when it's all over. Can't you leave me be?

MARY

You been laying there like that ever since Rance and Dan went into town this morning.

OCIE

Well, maybe I need some rest. Besides, I have to think. If I say the wrong thing, I might not get my hands on

45

him. If I make a wrong move, something might happen. Buster Drumwright might get away from me or holler. I don't want to let nobody down tonight.

MARY

If you do it, Ocie, you'll let us all down. You'll let yourself down, too. Think about Kathleen . . .

OCIE

What do you think I'm thinking about? Listen woman, I tried all I could to keep my brother from beating the daylights out of you. But you're pushing me too far. Always pushing, ain't you? Well, maybe I won't stop Dan the next time he takes it in his head to slap his wife around a little. Maybe that's what you been needing, a good whipping.

MARY

You don't mean that. I know you don't mean it, Ocie.

OCIE (*Fiercely*)

You just wait and see if I don't mean it. Hear me! You just wait. All the time trying to talk us out of doing what we must. Listen woman, we been wronged. We had a terrible thing to happen to our family, and if you had any backbone, if you was really a member of this family—I mean if you was really a Hedgepath—then you'd see. Then you'd quit all this mousy talking.

MARY

I can't stand by silent and see you do this thing, not and be a Christian, I can't. Ocie, don't do it. I've been praying for you not to do it. They're going to hang Buster Drumwright anyway.

46

OCIE

You just don't understand. You don't have no reasoning about you. This *Bible's* made you blind, ain't it? If it was your sister, your Kathleen, you'd be singing a different tune. You'd be mad, and you'd want to go down there and kill him yourself. You'd see red just like Dan, like your own husband does. Well, at least you can leave me alone.

MARY

Ocie . . .

(*Ocie sits up on the edge of the cot.*)

OCIE

You want me to betray my own brothers, don't you? Well, listen, I went off from here when I was thirteen, and I never hit a lick to support my family. Paw was dead then, and I never even come home to see my maw buried . . .

MARY

Ocie . . .

(*She looks at him pleadingly, close to tears.*)

OCIE

I never even knew she was dead—my own maw. Then my only sister married some no-count ridgerunner, and still no Ocie. I was gone off, roaming this world that whole time, all them years! They could have starved to death for all I knowed. Maybe if I'd stayed home and worked, none of it would have happened. But I was a dern bum—a drifter.

MARY

Killing Buster Drumwright is not going to help. It'll

47

only destroy us. It'll only wipe out what few of the Hedgepaths are left. They'll run us out of the country. We'll be scattered like the leaves in wintertime, Ocie.

OCIE

That's a plain lie. They'll thank us. They'll thank me. They'll say, Ocie Hedgepath finally come home and took over his family responsibilities. Ocie Hedgepath— they'll point at me—he defended his family's pride. I'll be what I never been before, what I ain't never been, not once in my whole life until this here night coming on—I'll be a hero.

MARY

You're thinking crazy. What's inside of you, I wonder, to make you think that way?

OCIE

You don't think it, woman—you feel it. Like Dan said, it burns like ashes in your chest. It makes you lay awake at night. It's your kin and your blood, and if you're a Hedgepath, you feel it in your veins. No, you ain't one of us. Dan's right.

MARY (*Turning toward the window*)

It's almost black dark. When will the boys be coming, I wonder? I been hoping all day this night wouldn't come. You don't know the dread that's in my bones.

OCIE

Take yourself away from me. Get on and fix our supper. You can do that, anyway.

MARY

Are you going to eat supper? I fixed it while you were asleep.

48

OCIE (*Lying down again, opening the Bible now*)
I don't know. I don't know if I will eat or not.

MARY (*At the window*)
I see a lantern on the path. It must be Dan and Rance.
I better set the vittles out.

(*She ties on her apron as heavy footfalls cross the porch outside and the two brothers enter.*)

DAN

Ocie? You better get up quick.

(*Ocie sits up, holding his place in the Bible.*)

MARY

Is anything wrong?

RANCE

They may get Buster before you do, Ocie.

OCIE (*Uncertainly*)
What?

DAN

It's a bunch from Knox County piled into town this evening. They've teamed up with some from this county, and they say they're going to take Buster Drumwright out and burn him. I talked to Fate Stanhope, and he said it was too many of them. Besides, he says he's tired of sitting up all night for three weeks. His nerves is shot, he said.

OCIE

You mean the deputy is going to let them take him?

RANCE

It looks that way. If they rush him, he's going to give over the keys. He says he can't rightly shoot nobody for the likes of Buster Drumwright. Leastways, he told

49

Dan that, just a minute ago. The mob was working up
to rush the jail whenever we left town.

OCIE (*Standing up and brushing off his clothes*)
I better get going.

MARY
You're not going down there, are you? What's the use?
Ocie? At least eat your supper. Ocie?
(*Ocie leaves.*)

DAN
We'll wait here, Ocie.
(*He goes to the door behind Ocie and looks out into
the darkness.*)
We'll be waiting!
(*He shouts into the night, after Ocie.*)
Get him, Ocie!

SCENE THREE

[DISSOLVE TO: The exterior of the jail]
(*Fate Stanhope stands on the porch, holding the gun
ready. The crowd mills around before him. Some of
them bear torches.*)

BYSTANDER
You may as well give over the keys to us, Fate. There
are too many of us now.

FATE
I'd hate to have to shoot you. I'd hate to have to shoot
any of you. Now put them torches away. Put them out
and go back home!

50

BYSTANDER

Don't make us burn down the jail to get him, Fate. Give us the keys.

CROWD

Burn the jail! Let's burn it down!

BUSTER

Don't worry, Fate. I wouldn't blame you if you gave them the keys.

FATE

What's come over you?

(*He pauses, sizing Buster up.*)

So you finally got afraid, eh? The great Buster Drumwright, the mad-dog killer!

BUSTER

Think what you please. I just said I wouldn't blame you none if you let them take me.

FATE

Well, I ain't going to give them the satisfaction, nor you, neither. I'm going to see that rope put on your neck good and legal.

(*We go close in on Buster's face as he looks down at the crowd. The torches flicker against the frame of the window and upon the heavy iron bars he grips.*)

BYSTANDER

Well, do you give us the keys, or do we have to take them off of you? Which is it gonna be?

(*Ocie mounts to the porch beside Fate Stanhope.*)

OCIE (*To Fate*)

Can I say something?

FATE

It won't do no good, Preacher.

51

BYSTANDER

You're too late, Preacher. We've made up our minds!

OCIE (*Addressing the mob*)

If you can just give me a minute . . .

BYSTANDER

You can have a minute, Preacher.

OCIE

Maybe you fellows don't understand something. I know how you feel about this man, but I also know some things about him you don't know. You see, I come all the way here from Texas just to save his soul. I come all that way just to bring probably the worst sinner in the world to Christ. I wanted him to have the good news before he died.

BYSTANDER

That's the truth. This preacher come all the way from Texas.

OCIE

I come down here tonight, it being the last night Buster Drumwright will be alive . . .

BYSTANDER

You're right there, Preacher!

OCIE

I come down here tonight in order to baptize him.
(*Turning to Fate Stanhope*)
Ain't that right, Deputy?

FATE

That's the gospel truth. It sure is.

OCIE

I can't baptize him after he's dead, can I?
(*Pausing, during which the crowd grows silent*)

So I'm asking you to do God a favor. I'm asking you to give me time to bring this man to Christ. I ain't trying to turn you from your purpose. I'm only a poor preacher, and I couldn't do that noways, no matter how hard I tried. But I come a long way to do this work . . .

FATE

How about it, boys?

BYSTANDER

Let's give the preacher a chance. I don't aim to interfere with God. Don't none of us aim that.

(*He removes his hat as an act of reverence, setting down his gasoline can and coiling the rope on top of it.*)

OCIE

Can you get some of them to bring the bathtub to the hall upstairs?

FATE

Sure, Preacher.

BYSTANDER

Come on, let's get that tub over yonder! A few strong backs, that's all that's needed.

(*We see Buster Drumwright's serene face at the cell window, then cut to Ocie, looking up and then turning to Fate Stanhope.*)

OCIE

If you'll let me in, I'll go up and get him ready.*

---

* USING sheet metal and wood, the bathtub for the CBS Television production was specially made. There was then the problem of how to fill the tub unfailingly to the proper depth for a baptism in so short a time. The Special Effects Department came to the rescue. A large tank of water on rubber

FATE (*Unlocking the door*)
It's a miracle, Preacher. A minute ago they was ready to lynch him.
(*Ocie starts up the steps. The tub is brought behind him.*)
BYSTANDER
(*He is laboring under his load. Fate Stanhope also bears a hand.*)
Easy does it. Don't drop her, boys!

SCENE FOUR

[DISSOLVE TO: Cell corridor inside the jail]
(*There is a close-up of Buster. We pull back to see the tub being filled by a bucket brigade. Ocie stands silently by, watching. He turns to look at Buster.*)
[THE END OF ACT TWO]

---

wheels was to roll onto the set and fill the tub to the right depth in five seconds.

When the show was taped the first time, the tank appeared on schedule and filled the tub. "Buster" stepped into it, and a look of pious horror came over his face. When "Ocie" laid hands on him and pushed him under the surface, Ocie's face in turn looked savagely grim. "Marvelous acting!" The murmur went through the control room like electricity. Then, to the surprise of everyone watching, Ocie suddenly hauled Buster up out of the tub. By a slight miscalculation, the water provided turned out to be scalding hot.

For the second taping, this oversight was corrected; lukewarm water was provided. The show came off as planned.

Act Three

[DISSOLVE TO: The cell corridor]
(*Throughout this scene, the sound of the tub being filled forms a background against which the conversation between Buster and Ocie is pitched. At first the buckets come rapidly. But toward the end they are spaced further and further apart, so that both men begin unconsciously to listen for the sound of water being poured into the tub, as the scene draws toward its close.*)

BUSTER

I knowed you was coming, Preacher.

OCIE

I never had no chance to ask you if you had decided to be baptized or not. I had to act sort of quick out yonder just now.

BUSTER

It taken a lot of guts to stand up in front of a bunch like that and beg for me. They might have shot you down. I know I've killed for less than that. What you done taken guts.

OCIE

I had a lot to gain by it, is why I done it. You are going to be baptized, ain't you, Buster?

BUSTER

You was going to tell me what happened to Paul, remember? After that I'll tell you if I am or if I ain't.

55

OCIE

That's fair and square.

BUSTER

How did he die, Preacher?

OCIE

Well, they trumped up this charge against him in Rome.

BUSTER

He was framed!

(*Ocie nods.*)

The dirty sapsuckers.

OCIE

So they handed down a verdict which was to throw him to the tigers and lions.

BUSTER

And did he take it all right?

OCIE

He never batted an eyelash. When they come and got him out of his cell, they didn't have to drag him.

BUSTER

He walked by his own self, didn't he? I knew he'd have acted that way.

OCIE

He had done been baptized, of course, and he knew there wasn't nothing to fear. He believed in Christ, and he knew where he was going.

BUSTER

And then what?

OCIE

So they got him to the edge of the pit where they kept

Fate Stanhope

Mary and Ocie
Hedgepath

Buster Drumwright,
Fate, and the mob

From the CBS Television production

Mary and Ocie

Ocie and Buster

Ocie and Buster

From the CBS Television production

these big hungry cats, and they was getting ready to push him, and he says, "Hold on. There won't hardly be any need for that." He wouldn't let them push him.

BUSTER

He didn't want them to, did he? They didn't have to push him.

OCIE

That's right. He looked them tigers and lions right in the eye.

(*Pausing, as a bucket of water is poured*)

They was roaring and snarling. And then . . . he jumped.

BUSTER

I knew it. I knew he had to have gone out something like that there. He went . . .

(*Pausing, as water is poured*)

. . . under his own steam, without nobody pushing and shoving at him.

OCIE

Here's something he wrote. I'll read it to you.

BUSTER

Let's hear it.

(*They wait while Fate Stanhope comes with a bucket of water. Fate pours it into the tub.*)

OCIE (*Reading haltingly, unsure of the words, but with rustic eloquence*)

"If ye then be risen with Christ, seek those things which are above, where Christ sitteth on the right hand of God. Set your affection on things above, not on things on the earth. For ye are dead . . .

57

(*He pauses as the Bystander brings a bucket of water up the corridor and pours it into the tub.*)

. . . and your life is hid with Christ in God. When Christ, who is our life, shall appear, then shall ye also appear with him in glory."

(*Ocie closes the Bible and looks up. Buster Drumwright is deeply moved.*)

BUSTER

I feel so awful, so bad about all the things . . . the sins I committed. I . . .

OCIE

It's the Holy Spirit in you, moving into your innards.

BUSTER

What was that last you read, the last part, ". . . then shall ye . . ."?

OCIE

"Then shall ye also appear with him in glory."

BUSTER

Did Paul . . . did he mean me when he wrote that there?

OCIE

He sure did. That's the good news.

BUSTER

But I don't deserve it. I killed. I murdered.

OCIE

Don't none . . .

(*Pausing as water is poured*)

. . . don't nobody deserve it, Buster. I been meaning to ask. You got any folks, any kin?

58

BUSTER

Me? Naw, Preacher. There won't be nobody to send after. Nobody would claim me.

OCIE

I thought maybe you had a sister or something.

BUSTER

A sister? Yeah, I had a sister, but I lost track of her long ago. We was orphaned, and Sis, she used to try to look out for me. I'd nearly forgot about her. Her given name was Sadie. She sure was a good thing, Sadie was. But even if you could find her, I wouldn't want her to know nothing until after . . .

(*Pausing*)

. . . after it's all over. I sure miss her right now, my Sis.

OCIE (*With irony*)

I know how you feel.

(*The Bystander pours the final bucket.*)

BYSTANDER

I believe that ought to be deep enough, boys.

FATE

Your tub's ready, Preacher.

BUSTER

And I miss Paul. I ain't never got over seeing him shot, laying there with his eyes open beside of me, and them Revenue men opening up on all sides . . .

BYSTANDER

If you don't mind, Deputy, me and some of the rest of the bunch would like to stay up here and watch the baptizing.

59

(*He stands reverently, with his hat in his hand. Ocie looks up in alarm as Fate Stanhope weighs the pros and cons. Close in on Fate's face, we see his momentary indecision.*)

FATE

Naw, I guess we better all clear out. Preacher, I'll leave you the key.

(*Handing the key to Ocie*)

This unlocks the cell door.

BYSTANDER

We'll be waiting outside, Preacher. Tell us when it's over.

OCIE (*Grimly*)

I will.

BYSTANDER

(*He has been leaving, walking down the hallway in front of the deputy. Now he stops.*)

And Preacher, I want to apologize for the rest—for me and the rest of us out yonder, for how we acted. We're ashamed of it now. You made us ashamed and . . . well, I'm proud to know a real man of God. That's all. I . . . I'm just proud.

(*Ocie stands speechless. The last two men are going down the steps as he turns to Buster and unlocks the door separating them. The door swings open, and Buster comes out wearing an expression of beatitude. Ocie puts out his hand, and Buster takes it. He is full of trust.*)

BUSTER

Wait a second.

OCIE

Just come this way.

(*But Buster stops halfway to the tub and pulls his hand away from Ocie's.*)

BUSTER

Something I want to say. I got a confession, sort of . . . what I mean is, before, when I hollered at that window . . . well, I was really scared. I was afraid, thinking about when they were going to put that rope around my neck. I got dizzy and weak just thinking about that morning—tomorrow it is, now. I could feel the rope choking me.

OCIE

(*He begins to show his impatience.*)

I know, brother. I know.

BUSTER

But you know what? I'm not afraid now. I know you'll be out there in that crowd, and I know I can look at your face, Preacher. It gives me strength to know I can depend on you.

(*With wonderment*)

Truly, I ain't afraid no more.

(*Ocie takes his hand and leads him to the tub. Buster steps into the tub.*)

OCIE

I guess you better sit down and sort of lay back. I'll need a good grip on you.

BUSTER (*Jokingly*)

Do a good job, Preacher.

(*He reclines in the tub, with his head just above the*

61

surface of the water. Ocie gets a good grip on him. His hands tighten on Buster's arms.)

OCIE

I baptize thee in the name of the Father and of the Son and of the Holy Ghost.

BUSTER *(Reciting)*

"Then shall ye also appear with him in glory."

OCIE *(Fiercely)*

Amen!

(He shoves Buster under the water with all his force and holds him there. His face is contorted with rage. But as the seconds tick away his arms begin to tremble. Suddenly his face relaxes with a wracking sound, almost a sob, and he draws Buster, gasping for air, up out of the water. Neither man speaks as Buster steps from the tub, still gasping. He looks at Ocie.)

BUSTER

You sure took me at my word whenever I said for you to do a good job of it! I thought for a minute . . . *(Pausing)*

You meant to drown me, didn't you, Preacher?

OCIE

I'll have to tell you who I am. I'm Ocie Hedgepath. I never was no preacher.

BUSTER *(Slowly comprehending)*

Hedgepath?

OCIE

My sister Kathleen and her baby.

(Now that the ordeal is over and he has confessed, Ocie sags a little.)

62

BUSTER

That was your sister and her baby—them?

OCIE

Yeah.

(*Ocie follows Buster back to the cell and closes the door as Buster steps inside it. He turns the key, locking Buster behind bars again.*)

BUSTER (*Anxiously*)

You . . . you still going to be there tomorrow, Preacher?

OCIE (*Reaching through the bars to put his hand on Buster's arm*)

I'll be there.

(*Withdrawing his arm, Ocie stoops down wearily and picks up the Bible from the floor where he laid it. Then he straightens up to stare at the tub in the hallway. Like the tub itself, he is somehow forlorn, but victorious. The scene fades out.*)

[THE END]

The Stage Script

Characters

BUSTER DRUMWRIGHT: A killer, twenty years old.
FATE STANHOPE: A deputy sheriff, twenty years old.
OCIE HEDGEPATH: A drifter, about thirty-five years old.
RANCE HEDGEPATH: Ocie's brother, a millhand, twenty-four years old.
DAN HEDGEPATH: Ocie's brother, also a millhand, twenty-two years old.
MARY HEDGEPATH: Dan's wife, twenty-one years old.
BYSTANDER: Fat, about forty years old.
PREACHER: Thirty-two years old.
MOB LEADER
WOMAN
MAN
MOB

Scenes

ACT ONE

ACT TWO

Act One

SCENE ONE

[SETTING: The place is a small county seat in East Tennessee. The time is the early part of the twentieth century. It is midsummer. They have electric lights, but not the electric chair or the electric guitar. The set shows a dim, dark, violent age. It is the golden age of fundamentalist religion, white spiritual music, and the vengeful Anglo-Saxon Jehovah.

The unit set has a small jail at stage right. There is a porch set before a brick wall. The wall is scrim and has a window. When the jail exterior is dimmed and the interior is lit, we see a narrow cell at the left, barred off. A door of bars opens to the right into the somewhat wider cell block. The stark cell has two rough wooden stools. A door of bars opens to the right into the somewhat wider cell block. The cell block, in turn, has a steel security door at the right, letting out onto the porch. A glaring, unfrosted electric light hangs by a green cord from the ceiling of the cell block.

On the narrow jail porch there is an old chair. Off the porch, there is a fifty-gallon steel drum, in which a fire is lit during the chilly hours of night to warm Fate Stanhope during his continuous vigil. Ropes and harness hang on the porch stanchions.

At midstage is a narrow space of limbo with a surrealistic tree standing far back in dark outline against the cyclorama. It is a symbolic tree of life or a gallows —a symbol of vengeance.

At stage left is the Hedgepath cabin, with a door at the right, a narrow porch outside, and the remainder the interior. There is a ladder on the back wall, leading up to a sleeping loft with a curtained entrance. There is a fireplace in the left wall with an exit space up beyond it, at the left. The furnishings are sparse and primitive. Downstage at the left is a battered rocking chair. There is a round table with chairs about it and a window in the rear wall through which the cyclorama can be seen, showing night, or sunset, or dawn. Ocie's bed is a pallet, which he rolls out and arranges downstage when needed. The cabin lights are soft oil lamps, in contrast to the brash lights at the jail.

The playing area is lit dimly to create a sense of night and oppression, a cramping in of darkness. The part of the set not in use is totally dark.]

(*Behind the dim set, a five-string banjo plays* AIRLINE TO HEAVEN *in brassy Blue Grass style. Ralph Swiggert strolls out from up midstage, a minstrel outlined against the dark blue cyclorama. Lights catch him as he comes down, bareheaded, brightly dressed in a fancy shirt of many colors, slim trousers, and cowboy boots. He sings.*)

RALPH

"Sinner, hurry to the airport, your plane is leaving
    soon—

72

Not headed for no earthly place, not headed to the
  moon;
Taking you beyond the stars to a holy destination—
A one-way fare will git you there, to the land of your
  salvation.

CHORUS

Oh, the stewardess, she's an angel; the pilot, he's a
  saint;
And the runway, it is paved with solid gold;
There's no need for navigation, the Good Book shows
  the way.
Sinner, hurry for the day is growing old,
Sinner, hurry for the day is growing old."
(*He winds up with a flourish of chords.*)

Some of you may recognize me—Ralph Swiggert?
Maybe seen me while I traveled in foreign lands with
that great woman evangelist, Minnie Mayfair Mundine,
playing gospel hymns for her on this very banjo. And
let me tell you, friends—praise the Lord!—let me tell
you, we brung many a sorry unwashed heathen sinner
to the Lord in them backwoods countries overseas. Me
and Minnie went across the water, and we saved them
wretches in droves.

Drove them crazy with this banjo, like a hypnotizer,
and Minnie coming in with her words—that's how
Minnie done it, with words. Words come out of her
mouth in sweet swarms like bees, and each one had a
stinger to it, and my music a-luring and a-luring them
on, whether they talked American or not. It didn't

73

make no difference. They come on anyway, like thirsty herds of cattle after water. My God, I can still remember the awful smell of their salvation. Friends, the greatest part of them people over yonder eats a great deal of garlic and takes a very few baths.

Anyway, this here, tonight, this here was a good while back, after I left my wife and took up gospel-playing with Minnie Mayfair Mundine, after I left my wife—praise the Lord!—to follow my heart and help to save the filthy foreign heathen, as well as quite a few hundred percent Americans in this here country. Amen. This here was back before the electric chair and the electric guitar, but *after* the electric lights come in, back before the curse of foreign aid laid its blight upon our substance, in other words, back when a dollar was a buck and not just twenty-five cents and when whiskey and cigarettes wasn't priced out of all sane reason.

Praise the Lord, God give man the scriptures, but I know the Devil give man whiskey and cigarettes just to run the price of them up and torture the poor. Well, I give up both whiskey *and* cigarettes long before whiskey was making folks alcoholics and cigarettes was giving people the cancer—back when a cigarette was still just a smoke and whiskey didn't create nothing worse than drunks—give them both up, along with my wife, Kathleen Hedgepath, in order to follow Minnie Mayfair Mundine and play the Lord's music. It was also back when a bum was something they dropped out of airplanes—on *other* people.

Ralph Swiggert, that's me, and you are welcome to

send your twenty-five–cent dollars, any contributions, large or small, to Ralph, that's R-A-L-P-H, Box 99, Juarez, Mexico, to keep this ministry spreading. Remember that Ralph ain't to blame for none of this here. (*He waves at the stage behind him.*)
Watch it close. See the scriptures, see the book, my friends, and just remember that, whether you want to think about it or not, all our kin started in that book with this Jewish fellow, Adam, and his wife, Mistress Eve. You know what she done in cahoots with a snake. And remember the great flood and everything else, on down through several race riots and ten thousand crooked county elections. Praise the Lord!

It's God versus the Devil in a fight to the finish. Yes, folks, them's our two main amusements right today—killing murderers and helping with the spread of the gospel, the good news. It's show business, folks, a major industry, but—praise the Lord!—my time's up. I got to go. But you go to Tennessee some summer night, and you listen up in them hills, listen right close, and you might hear a banjo playing something like this here.
(*He begins softly playing* MANSIONS IN THE SKIES.)

Playing, eh? Might be me a-playing, or some other man a-playing, or God—it might be God out there all alone on the mountaintop, playing what's in the heart of us every one.

God bless and keep you all, every one. Amen!
(*He bows and goes off, still playing in the Blue Grass style. The music is drowned out as the mob comes on, yelling in anger. They carry ropes, cans, staves, and*

75

jugs. They surge forward toward Fate Stanhope, who forces them back with his gun. As they fall back after the rush at Fate, Ocie appears upstage right and slowly approaches. He is notable for not carrying any implement, and for his quietness. The sullen mob recoils and is silent, foiled for the instant. Buster comes to the window and stands up on one of the stools in his cell to look out.)

BYSTANDER

Come on, let us have him, Fate! There you are, you dang little murderer! We going to burn you, Drumwright!

BUSTER

You tell 'em, fat boy!

OCIE

So that's Buster Drumwright.

BYSTANDER

That's him. And we're going to pour gasoline on him and set it afire.

OCIE

You aim to lynch him.

BYSTANDER

That's right. Comes a time when decent folks got to act to protect law and order. All right, Fate! How about it! Do you give him to us, or do we come after him?

FATE

Now, I already told you, the legal hanging's in three days. Now back up!

76

BYSTANDER

You wouldn't shoot honest folks to protect a murderer, Fate. You wouldn't gun down fellow Christians. You ain't fooling nobody, kid!

FATE

I warned you once! Now get back. Ain't nobody taking this prisoner from me.

BYSTANDER

You're acting a fool, Fate. Listen, boy . . .

FATE

I got my orders. This hanging's going to be fair and legal. Can't you wait three days? What's the rush?

BUSTER

Let 'em come. Come get me, fat boy! Come on, try it. Bunch of knife-swappers, that's all you are!

FATE

Shut up, Buster! Now get down away from that window and hush. You just riling them up.

BYSTANDER

All right, let's take him!

(*Fate shoots over the heads of the mob.*)

You would *shoot,* wouldn't you?

FATE

I told you. I got my orders. I'd hate to kill anybody, but you done pushed me too far. So now git! All of you! Git!

BUSTER

That's it! Tuck your tails. Run! Run away, you sawed-off bunch of buzzards.

77

WOMAN

Listen at him blackguarding! Hold your blackguarding tongue, Buster Drumwright!

FATE

Buster, I already said shut up! Now get out of that window. Go on now!

OCIE

So that's him. Buster Drumwright.

(*This scene is played to the audience as frank exposition.*)

BYSTANDER

Yes sir, and you better believe we had lots of important people coming from far and near to get a look at him. No argument about it, there stands the most notorious killer in the history of Tennessee—in *our* jail! There stands the killer of seventeen people, including two niggers and some children.

OCIE

Buster Drumwright, the murderer.

BYSTANDER

You might be a stranger to these parts, I don't know. But Buster Drumwright has been wrote up all over the country in the news. Ain't he?

WOMAN MOB MEMBER

He ain't lying to you, fellow.

MAN

Yeah, we ended a pretty dang large hunt when we caught him.

OCIE

You helped catch him?

78

BYSTANDER

All of us! Why man, the whole town of Trammel turned out! You bet your life! Miss Betty Bruce Baxter, here she come running into Horace's grocery . . .

MAN

We was just sitting around minding our business, you know . . .

BYSTANDER

And Miss Betty comes in a-yelling, "Somebody's robbing the bank!"

MAN

Horace Stallings's store, yonder next to the bank.

BYSTANDER

So we jump up and grab every gun Horace has in stock. When Drumwright comes backing out of that bank, we're in the street waiting, and brother, we open fire! We declare war on him.

WOMAN

You never heard so much shooting!

MAN

And tell about the underwear salesman . . .

BYSTANDER

Yeah. It's this ladies' underwear salesman out of Knoxville. Buster has captured this man and his car to bring him up here to Trammel, to rob our bank. Only we don't know none of this.

WOMAN

Let me tell him. See, Buster come out with the salesman, and don't none of us know it's Buster, and don't nobody know it's a salesman. Time like that, every-

79

body figures it's just two plain old Saturday afternoon bank robbers.

BYSTANDER

Right! So here they come out the bank and jump in the salesman's car. The salesman, he tries to drive it off, only we done shot every dang tire off that car, so it moves kind of slow. So I run up alongside the car by the driver's side and shoot the underpants salesman in the face. I mean I give it to him! And he quits driving. But Buster jumps out of the car and runs off towards the railroad tracks shooting at us . . .

MAN

With a German pistol.

OCIE

He hit anybody?

WOMAN

Did he!

BYSTANDER

Let me tell *you!* It's Horace's store and Horace's guns. Horace has furnished every scrap of the ammunition only Horace don't have no gun hisself. Been so busy he's passed them all out and ain't saved one for hisself. So all Horace has is a garden hoe he's yanked up out of stock, and he's chasing along with the rest of us, when he sort of falls flat, like a sack of feed, hoe and all.

WOMAN

Nobody paid him much nevermind when he fell.

MAN

Well, I saw Horace. But I figured he'd done tripped

Osborne Robinson's set design for the stage production

From the Vanderbilt University Theater production

on his shoe laces or something. I mean, you don't have no time to stop at a time like that.

OCIE

Buster got him?

BYSTANDER

In the chest. Little bitty hole size of your little finger. Horace made number seventeen for Buster Drum-wright.

OCIE

Horace Stallings dead. A German pistol.

BYSTANDER

Yeah. A fine fellow. Maybe you knew him.

WOMAN

Don't forget the salesman!

BYSTANDER

Well, now I never had time to look when Horace fell, like he (*indicating the Man*) told you. Because I've just shot this salesman, and he's coming out of the car waving a white handkerchief, so they say.

WOMAN

He was. I seen him waving it when he come out of the car.

BYSTANDER

That's what they all say. Well, blood is running all over him. He's a terrible sight. You can't be too sure, I say, in a case like that, so I pour it on him again. Shot him twice more until somebody hollers he's trying to surrender. I'm awful sorry I done it when I find out he's innocent. Just Buster's hostage, you know.

81

MAN

Well, it's like I told him. I says, "Fellow, we all make mistakes, every one of us makes a mistake now and then." I told him, I said, "Fellow we ain't no different. We're sorry, but that's how it is." He just laid there on the ground, still trying to wave that handerchief.

OCIE

Did he live?

BYSTANDER

The pants man? Sure. In the hospital down at Knox-ville, doing just fine.

MAN

The salesman? The hostage?

BYSTANDER

Yeah.

MAN

I heard yesterday the doctors think maybe he'll walk again if they fix him up with the right kind of leg brace. Was *you* the one shot him?

BYSTANDER

Well, I ain't going to claim *all* the credit. But now I hit what I shoot at! Maybe some more shot him too—but I'll have to say I was the main one all right. Had no way to know he was innocent, so I poured it on him, sure! But it's either you or him, don't you see?

OCIE

But everybody missed Buster.

MAN

Hell, *he* dodged like a quail. Naw. Horace fell, and Buster run out of ammunition about then and jumped in a ditch yonder by the railroad. Crawled up in the culvert, so we sent back to the store for dynamite. We're fixing to blow him out of there. I had already struck the match, only here comes the sheriff sticking his nose in it. Never had no chance to do justice ourselves. The sheriff locked him up.

MOB MEMBER

Makes you sick.

MAN

And it wasn't till way up in the next day they found out who they had.

WOMAN

The next day before they knew he was Buster Drumwright. I tell you, our town ain't been the same since. Honest folks can't hardly sleep at night!

BYSTANDER

We was the ones risked our necks catching him! And when I think of all the lowdown things he's done! You just about wore out our patience, Deputy!

MOB

Yeah! What're we waiting for! Get him!

FATE

Don't make me shoot! Official public hanging's three days off! Fair and legal now! Just three more days.

BYSTANDER

Hand him over!

MAN

Hand him over!

WOMAN

Now we mean business, Stanhope!

(*The stage dims out.*)

SCENE TWO

[SETTING: The Hedgepath cabin. It is the same night.] (*Dan and Rance sit with Mary about the table. The Preacher is standing, exhorting them. Ocie comes stealthily to the door and listens, standing on the cabin porch.*)

PREACHER

The whole town feels the way you do, boys. But we can't have the sin and stain of a lynching on our hands. We profess to be Christians, after all. Now I didn't want to do it, what I had to do today . . .

RANCE

Easy for you to talk. Easy for you to say forgive him, sure. But what about us? Our own sister, the best woman who ever walked on God's earth . . . Kathleen —killed!

DAN

And her baby. Preacher, you take anybody that would murder a woman and her baby. And he killed them, Preacher! Our own flesh and kin!

RANCE

All right, Dan. Get a hold on yourself. The Preacher come up here to help us.

PREACHER

I know how you feel, boys. Believe me when I say I know. But if we believe Christ is our savior . . . I didn't want to do what I had to do this morning. But I'm a Christian. And that's why I went to see Buster Drumwright today.

84

DAN

You mean you went inside the jail and saw him, Preacher?

PREACHER

It was my duty to see if I could help prepare him to meet God. So I saw him, but it wasn't any use. Drumwright cursed me and laughed at me. Why, he's like . . . a devil!

RANCE

That's him. You take anybody that would kill a woman and a baby, a sweet small child that never drank nothing stronger than milk and never knew no sin! It just . . . just breaks something down inside me.

PREACHER

Breaks anybody down to think of it, Rance—anybody. But lynching is something else again!

RANCE

Lynching is too good for him. Too quick and easy!

PREACHER

Well, you can't say that. But I will say I stood out there this morning watching them build the gallows. A lot of good workmanship went into it, I can tell you. And every plank they nailed down was a comfort to my heart. Yes it was! I said *Amen* with every hammerstroke, and it did me good to see Buster Drumwright looking out his window, watching that good work going forward. *Amen,* that's what I said, boys! But now, now we got to be Christians, and you must hold this thought in your hearts. Try to remember what

85

I'm going to tell you, Rance. *God* will punish Buster Drumwright, and he can do a better job at it than anybody in this room.

DAN

God! What kind of a God lets a family's only sister die for no good cause? You think I ain't thought about that, Preacher?

MARY

Dan, Dan! Please hush.

PREACHER

God's ways are a mystery. God *will* punish Buster Drumwright, Dan. Just remember that. Shall we have prayer?

(*He closes his eyes, his face turned upward. Mary stands bowed, following the words of the prayer with humble, close attention. Dan and Rance somewhat reluctantly go through the motions of prayer, although with some show of impatience.*)

O Lord God, Heavenly Father, God of Mercy, God of Forgiveness, help us, we pray, to wipe all hatred and all desire for vengeance from our hearts. Especially do we ask you to help this family, the Hedgepaths. We ask you to help Dan and his dear wife, Mary, to accept the wisdom of thy ways and to live together under this roof in harmony and peace. Give Dan and Mary the blessing of children. And, O God, we ask that you help Rance. For he is the older brother, and with their daddy dead, Rance Hedgepath is now the head of this house and has many responsibilities and duties which weigh heavy upon his shoulders. Above all, O God, help us to understand in this time of trouble that a desire for vengeance will do us no good. Help our little community to understand this truth in this time of crisis! Now we don't know much about Buster Drumwright, O Lord. We don't know where he came from. We don't know why he had to cause so many people so much worry and trouble and sorrow. But we do think we know where Buster Drumwright is going, God, we pray that Wednesday morning, when they slip that noose around his sinner's neck, it will come to Buster too, just where it is he's eternally headed for, because of all his wicked crimes. And finally, bring all Christians to salvation in the end. We pray in the name of Jesus Christ. Amen.

(The group relaxes from its posture of prayer. The preacher quickly changes from his tone of pomposity in the prayer to one of easy pleasantry.)

Things going along all right up at the mill, eh, boys? I went by to call on the superintendent in his new house today. He and Mrs. Turner were packing for a trip to the ocean beach in South Carolina. Seems Turner don't relish having his young 'uns see the hanging. Left this morning. Now I thought it would do them good to see it.

MARY

Never seen the ocean. Always wanted to see it.

PREACHER

Not a great many has seen it, Mary. Say, you ought to see Mr. Turner's new house. Indoor bathroom, everything. It's an inspirational experience just to see what

87

all Mr. Turner has. Well. Goodbye. Praise the Lord!
*(Mary follows the Preacher outside. Ocie hides in the
shadows.)*

MARY

Thank you, Preacher. You got Dan to listen. I been so
afraid!

PREACHER

You got to rely on your faith, Mary. You got to realize
God is helping. A pretty young woman must never
lose her faith in God, not for one single minute. We're
in God's hands all the time. The scriptures say: "Be-
hold therefore the goodness and severity of God." Be-
hold His goodness, Mary, and have faith!

MARY

But you don't know how awful it's been, Preacher. I
just can't tell you . . .

PREACHER

Faith, Mary! I'll be back and pray with you again.
I'll come back. Goodnight.

MARY

Preacher . . .
(She comes back inside the cabin.)

DAN

Is that son of a bitch left?

RANCE

Hush! Let him get gone a ways!

DAN

High and mighty bastard! He can talk about the jury
and the gallows. It ain't his sister laying dead and
buried.

88

MARY

But you ain't still aiming to do it! Dan!

DAN

I told you to keep out of what ain't none of your affairs. Now listen to me, woman! You going to hush?

MARY

I'm your wife, ain't I, Dan? Like the Preacher said . . .

DAN

The Preacher said, the Preacher said! The Preacher said I might have to slap hell out of you, less'n you hush! The Preacher said! Here we are in trouble, full of trouble, and you can't shut up talking about what some preacher says.

OCIE

No call to slap her, Dan. She'll keep her mouth shut.

RANCE

Ocie! Wasn't I just wondering when you'd be back. The preacher just now went through some rigmarole about forgiving Buster Drumwright—all that religion crap.

OCIE

I heard him. I was hiding out yonder. It was a good prayer, though.

DAN

Oh, he can pray all right. Some preacher! Always full of advice about what ain't none of his business. Well, how was it? Did you think up a plan?

OCIE

It was like you said. A bunch hanging around outside with ropes and jugs of gasoline. It's only the deputy,

Fate Stanhope. He's all that's between them and Buster Drumwright. I got up so close that them two barrels on his shotgun looked like a couple of caves. Then I looked up at him and . . . I couldn't hardly believe it was the same fellow, little old Fate Stanhope. Why Fate was just a kid, maybe five years old when I left here. But he stood down there tonight on that jail porch holding that shotgun—big as a bear almost. It was like somebody throwed ice water on me. A shiver passed through me when it hit me how long I been away. All them years hit me.

RANCE

They recognize you, Ocie?

OCIE

Naw. Not a soul. Guess they've forgot there ever was a kid named Ocie Hedgepath. And fact of the business, I didn't hardly know none of them. They said Horace Stallings was dead.

DAN

Yeah, Horace got it the day they caught Buster. That's right.

OCIE

Horace was my age, my friend.

RANCE

He growed up to be a fat man, Ocie, real stout and quiet. Everybody liked him.

OCIE

It give me an awful feeling. Made me think of Paw and the old store where we traded whenever we went into town. I looked for it. That store's gone. It's a filling

90

station on that corner now. And everything was littler. Everything was all shrunk.

DAN

Yeah. But you come back at a good time, Ocie—when your family needed you. It's all three of us in this thing together now, ain't it, Ocie? The Hedgepath boys, together from now on.

RANCE

Like when we was kids. When Kathleen was . . . was alive. I keep remembering . . . how she would sit sewing in that corner there, by the fire.

DAN

Yeah. And recall what a pretty voice she had? Sometimes at night I dream I hear her singing. Then it comes to me what happened, and I start to grieving and hurting inside, all over again. I get right sick at heart.

OCIE

You never said just how it happened, how Buster Drumwright done it.

RANCE

It was a mighty hard thing, Ocie. Kathleen was living up yonder on the ridge. We built her a place up there when she married. She stayed up there alone with her baby and wouldn't leave that cabin and come back to us after her husband run away from her. She was too proud. So, it was the dead of last winter, and Drumwright must have come and begged her to let him in to warm by the fire, and then, when he got inside, begged her to fix him some supper. Knowing Kathleen, I guess she took pity on him. Buster was cold, and

91

she took him in and warmed him. Buster was hungry, so she fed him. She took pity . . .

(*He stops, filled with emotion. He continues, starting from a controlled tone, ending in anguished grief.*)

Well, the plates was still on the table when I got there. Buster Drumwright had took a knife and . . .

(*He pauses.*)

Kathleen and her baby boy was both laying there . . . and the cold wind! The cold wind was blowing through that open door. . . . The wind! And their innocent blood!

OCIE

So he done it with a knife. I heard it in Galveston, Texas, in this barbershop. This fellow read the newspaper out loud, how Buster Drumwright was caught and had confessed all them things. I didn't get no haircut. I lit out right then and come home. Only . . . only I never knew he done it with no knife!

DAN

(*He draws out his own knife and opens it.*)

Well then, how we going to get him? Ain't we been over it a hundred times already? Listen, if we don't hurry, that bunch down at the jail might beat us to him! After tonight, we got just two more nights—just two!

OCIE

Yeah. But you'll never get past Fate Stanhope's shotgun. That kid's just dumb enough to shoot. The only rush I saw they made at him—why, he shot over their heads. Somebody would be bound to get hurt. We couldn't get past that shotgun, I can tell you that.

DAN

Naw, I guess you're right, none of *us* could. And yet
. . . the Preacher, he went down there. And they let
him right in the jail, easy as you please—he said so
here tonight.

RANCE

And then he comes up here to talk *forgiveness*. Praying! Do I feel like praying when the son of a bitch
that killed Kathleen is laying at ease down there in
that jail? I got to do something about it. I don't know
how you all feel, but I got to do something now!
I *got* to!

DAN

Then let's go! We'll shoot Fate Stanhope off them
front steps if we have to. We'll just shoot . . .

OCIE

Hold on, now. It's enough in this family been killed
already. It's no need of any more getting killed.

DAN

Ocie, you ain't afraid, are you? Don't you want this
insult wiped off our name?

OCIE

Listen a minute. Now what you said—that preacher,
he got in to see Buster Drumwright because *he* was a
preacher. A preacher could get him!

RANCE

That's right. A preacher is one thing they can't refuse.
They just can't refuse a preacher.

DAN

A preacher! A preacher wouldn't have the guts. Besides,
we ain't got one.

RANCE

But we do, we have got one. They'd never suspect . . .

DAN

Him? That just left here? You gone crazy, Rance?
(*He pauses, slowly turning toward Ocie.*)
Ocie! Will you try it, Ocie?

OCIE

I don't look like a preacher. But if I could get into
the jail I could . . .

DAN

You could get him! You can *pretend* like you're a
preacher.

RANCE

All in the world you need is a Bible.

MARY

This is wrong. Don't imitate a preacher, Ocie. It's blasphemy.

DAN

Get out your Bible, Mary. We need it for Ocie—for
Brother Ocie. Go on now, get your Bible! Hear me,
woman!

MARY

Oh, Dan. Dan, don't do it! You just can't. God sees
what you're doing!
(*During this speech, she has taken out her Bible and
stands with it clutched to her breast.*)

DAN

If you're so damned set against it, it's bound to work!
Give it here!
(*He snatches the Bible away from her and gives it to
Ocie.*)

94

Here's our Bible, Brother Ocie. *Your* Bible.

OCIE

They say you got to be called to preach. The Lord calls you in some way. You might be walking down the road or catching a fast freight or just laying in a ditch asleep, maybe drunk. You might be picking peaches in Georgia or packing melons in Florida—you might be anywhere. And the Lord lays his hand on you. That's what I always heard.

RANCE

Ocie, I'll be damned if you don't *look* like a preacher. Don't he, Dan? Look at how he holds the book. It's how you hold it, Ocie, just like it was full of dynamite caps or something. Like it was so full of powder it's about to go off and blow somebody to hell any minute! Well, don't he, Dan? Don't he really sort of look like one?

DAN

By gum, I believe he does. It's going to work. It is! By gum, it's going to work!

RANCE

Whoa, now! Not so fast. We can't get excited. We got to be calm. We got to be like steel and brass. It has to be just another job of work. You got to fool Fate Stanhope, and he ain't going to be easy to fool. We got to think. And it's got to be done quiet. No yelling . . .

OCIE

All right, just give me a good sharp knife. The best way is to do Buster like he done Kathleen. I'll grab a quiet hold on his mouth and then just drop his guts

95

out on the jail floor. I'll carve Buster Drumwright just like a turkey. One slice at a time . . .

DAN

Yeah! A good knife? Take mine.

RANCE

Put the knife up. The knife's out.

DAN

What?

RANCE

I said no knife. Take if Fate searched Ocie. What's a preacher toting a knife like that for? I say all Ocie needs is his hands. Your hands. Just get them on his throat, and they'll spring together like a bear trap. You can strangle him real slow. The preacher's *hands,* if you see what I'm driving at.

OCIE

I see it now. Why would I want the knife, anyway? I'll just think of Kathleen. I'll think what he done to her and that baby boy. And then, before Buster Drumwright can say Jack Robinson, my hands will strike like two snakes and fasten on his throat and . . . and crush his life right out of him. I can feel the power coming in to them. These hands will do it! They will!

RANCE

Go along then. Time's getting away from us. You got to get him for us, Ocie!

OCIE

I'll get him. I'll get him.

MARY

Ocie, come back!

96

DAN (*To Ocie*)

Get him, Ocie!

(*He turns to Mary.*)

Trash! That's all I married. No principles, no sense!
No idea of what's right and what's wrong.

MARY

Dan, you got to stop him. God . . . God sees!

DAN

For the last time, leave God out of this! This ain't none
of God's God-damned business! You got that straight?
This is *Hedgepath* family business.

RANCE

Let me talk to her, Dan.

DAN

She needs the hell beat out of her. Talk won't help.
She's just . . . just without no common sense. She ain't
had no raising, no upbringing. She don't know the
first thing about family and kin and . . . and killing.
All she's got is God on her brain all the time. I'm
just going to have to beat her like a damned . . .
mule . . . or something.

(*Dan starts toward Mary in a rage. Rance grabs him
to protect Mary.*)

MARY

Rance, go tell Ocie to come back! Fetch him back,
Rance! He's your brother. Don't you care? Rance!
Please! God help us!

DAN

You don't have no common sense! So I'm going to
beat some into you. I can't have my wife to think like
some preacher's slut. I can't stand it.

97

RANCE

You're wasting your time, Dan. Mary's just a woman, and women can't help it sometimes, what they do. I talked to her before, ain't I? Let me explain it to her.

DAN

Why won't she listen at *me?*

RANCE

I can tell her so she'll understand. A man can't tell his wife nothing. You ought to at least know that much by now.

DAN

Tell her then! Tell her my sister's dead! Tell her Kathleen Hedgepath will never draw the breath of life again because of a dirty little son of a bitch that had to kill her!—that's laying down in that jail right now, tonight!

MARY

We'll meet Kathleen later on—upstairs in heaven, the baby too.

DAN

See there? Hear that? Now she's talking about heaven! All right, you talk to her. And then if you ain't done any good, I'll let that stick of stovewood talk to her a while. Fist-talk, that's all she can understand.

(*Dan climbs into the loft.*)

MARY

You wouldn't go after Ocie. Why?

RANCE

You know better than that. When your folks died and you didn't have clothes on your back nor bread in your

98

mouth nor a pillow to lay your head on—then you weren't too proud to take our help! Who was it took you in, Mary? Did God drop bread and warm clothes out of the sky, Mary? Or did the Hedgepath family take you in? Did God marry you and give you half of all he had in the world, or was it my brother? Was it Dan Hedgepath who's laying up in the loft yonder and his mind so worried over you he's almost raving crazy?

MARY

But the Preacher . . .

RANCE

Maybe the Preacher put clothes on your back. Maybe he married you, and that's why you can't have no loyalty for us. No pride, no honor! Ain't I been a good brother to you?

MARY

Yes, and that's why you have to go after Ocie and stop him. That's why I can't keep quiet, Rance, and see the family destroyed. Take revenge on Buster Drumwright, and you're no better than he is. Have murder in your heart, and you're the same as dead.

RANCE

It ain't murder. It's killing, but it ain't murder, you hear? It's like war. Yeah, it's the same thing as loving your country—but it's closer than that—it's loving your family till its means something. And when your kin is wronged, then you go out and you get revenge on them.

MARY

Rance, think of Jesus! We're Christians, witnesses for Christ. You confessed his name, and they buried you

99

with him in baptism. He commanded us to love our enemies and to forgive people who hurt us. You know what the Bible tells us, Rance! You know, Rance.

RANCE

This ain't no time to think about Christ. When something like this happens, you don't think nothing. You just do what people have always and always done way on back. Back before anybody remembers! But something remembers—you don't have to think, because you know what you have to do, and Jesus don't have no place in it. The time comes, and you got to forget Jesus and remember your kin. You're a Hedgepath. You got to set the Lord to one side till it's all over. If you can't do that when the time comes, then you ain't worth pig tracks! Hear me—pig tracks!

MARY

Last night I prayed for us all. "Vengeance is mine; I will repay, saith the Lord." I couldn't stop reading the Bible.

(*She opens the Bible and reads.*)

It says: "Therefore if thine enemy hunger, feed him; if he thirst, give him drink; for in so doing thou shalt heap coals of fire upon his head. Be not overcome of evil, but overcome evil with good."

RANCE

Sure, it reads nice! But you didn't walk up that hill last winter to Kathleen's cabin, through the snow. I come to the door, I step in, and all I see for a minute is blood, my own kin's blood, on the walls and the floor and the table. Then I see Kathleen, that never left my bedside when I was sick. But it ain't nothing I can do for her. Then I look around and find the baby. Laying against the wall like a broken doll! Don't read your scriptures to me! I don't know what I may do I might be sorry for later!

MARY

Rance, please! This ain't helping things! Rance, pray! Ask God for strength!

RANCE

Dig a hole! The ground's froze, and I taste blood where I've bit my tongue to keep the heart from bursting clean out of my chest! Did a hole in the ground, woman! And lay my own flesh and her own baby in it! Kathleen! Listen! Kathleen? We'll get him, Kathleen! You hear? We'll get him for you!

MARY

"Our Father which art in heaven, Hallowed be thy name. . . ."

RANCE

Damn you, hush!

MARY

What . . . what if they kill Ocie? You got to think, Rance!

RANCE

Kill Ocie? Ain't you got bat sense? If they kill Ocie, then I'll go, and if they kill me, then Dan will go—but somebody will get Buster Drumright. One of us will, you hear! Hedgepath hands will get him!

MARY

Christ Jesus, have mercy! Rance don't know what he's doing. He don't know what he's saying. You got to help him, Lord.

101

RANCE

Go on, get out! Go before—before I do something. You ain't one of us. So git! God made a mistake and let you marry into this family! Well, now you can fix up God's mistake.

(*He shoves her.*)

MARY

No, it ain't God's fault. I love Dan. And anyhow, marrying is for better or worse. My place is here, to the end. It's my place to fight, and it ain't my place to run. No place to run to, no woods with big hollow trees to hide in . . .

RANCE

No sense. You got no sense. This Christ business has you ruint.

MARY

What's happening to me? Why is everything all gone wrong? Nothing's right anymore like it was meant to be.

(*She calls to Dan. He appears and starts down from the loft.*)

Dan? Dan, ain't I tried to be a good wife? Ain't I cooked and mopped and ironed and washed and swept and toted my share? Ain't we laid close and kept warm the coldest nights?

DAN

Can't you see my mind's worried?

MARY

You don't have any recollection, Dan?

DAN

Oh, I remember! I remember when Kathleen was alive,

102

too. I remember back before, when that banjo-picking peckerwood she married hadn't run off yet. Ralph Swiggert, I remember him—and that's another son of a bitch I'm going to kill if I can just ever catch him. If he hadn't run away, my sister would still be living tonight. But hell naw, Ralph Swiggert and that damned banjo just blowed away one day like the wind. But I'll get him, I'll get him yet! I won't forget to do that! I laid down, but all I could wonder about was Ocie. I can't ponder on Ralph till we get Buster. After Buster, Ralph comes next, but I will say there's two kinds of men. It's one that's soft as honey and worth about what red dirt's bringing by the pound, that drinks whiskey and sings and picks the banjo, like Ralph Swiggert. And the other kind is me, and I'm the kind you married. And I'm going to always do what a Hedgepath must, if it takes the *hide*. You hear me what I'm saying? The *hide!* Killing, most of all, if it happens to be right!

MARY

God said, thou shalt not kill. What about God's law?

DAN

Don't argue with blood. You can't. Not you, not God, not anybody else. Blood always talks louder than you can holler, because blood is what you are. Blood! Kin, family, me!

MARY

You can't argue with Christ's blood. His blood is what you can't argue with, Dan.

DAN

Shut up. Just shut up! I don't want no more argument

103

on it, you hear? I'm thinking about Ocie going down there alone! I can't hardly stand not knowing nothing! Maybe I could just run down to the jail and see. He'll be getting there in a minute or two. Maybe I could help.

RANCE

You'll just mess it up. Sit down. This is one time you've got to wait. We all got to wait, because it's nobody else to depend on now but Ocie.

DAN

Man, wasn't I glad to see him, Rance? Wasn't it a fine thing Ocie come back home like he did?

(*The stage dims out.*)

SCENE THREE

[SETTING: The jail. It is the same night.]

(*Fate is seated on the porch. He is suddenly startled as Ocie approaches.*)

FATE

Hold it right there, fellow.

OCIE

I didn't mean to startle you.

FATE

You better watch how you sneak up on people! My job is saving Buster Drumwright for the legal gallows, Mister, and I aim to do it. I thought I had run the last of you peckerwoods away from here.

104

OCIE

I ain't part of that bunch, Sheriff.

FATE

I ain't the sheriff. I'm only his nephew.

OCIE

I thought sure you was the sheriff, way you're taking it so serious. Way you stood them down out here. It taken guts to do your duty that way!

FATE

The sheriff, my uncle, he don't want no part of this, so it's why he stuck me out here. If he come down here hisself, it might cost him the next election. This way, folks only get mad at me. But I can stand it! I'm just his deputy, that's all.

OCIE

Well, whatever you are, I ain't up to no mischief. It must be rough on a man to guard a fellow like that. Sitting here all night, all alone, with nothing but crickets and moths to keep a fellow company.

FATE

This gun's plenty of company. Two nights more, and me and this gun can rest.

OCIE

Hanging's that soon? It don't leave me much time.

FATE

Don't give you much *time?* Time for what?

OCIE

To bring Buster Drumwright to the Lord. I aim to save Buster Drumwright, and it's why I come all the way from Texas. You see, I . . . I felt the call inside of me, the call to save him.

FATE

A preacher out walking around this time of night. I'd look for the Devil to be out prancing, but not no preacher . . .

OCIE

I come a long, long way.

FATE

All the way from Texas, eh? Well, you sure come a long way for nothing. Nobody could save Buster Drumwright. Get it through your head.

OCIE

God could. God could save him!

FATE

Well, I wouldn't say that *God* couldn't. I wouldn't hardly be willing to go that far, of course. But no preacher could bring a man like Buster to Christ. You got any idea about how many folks he's murdered? Do you, preacher?

OCIE

I ain't heard tell the exact figure, no, but . . .

FATE

Seventeen. Now that's seventeen he *remembers* about. It's other things he can't even remember—and he ain't sorry he done none of it. He ain't the least bit sorry. You can't save him, Preacher. We had preachers around here before. You might just as well get on back home to Texas. Our own Trammel County preachers already tried and had to give him up.

OCIE

But you got to let me try! I come all this long way,

106

the Lord calling me every step! Brother, won't you just let me *try?*

FATE

Come back tomorrow. See my uncle about it. He's sheriff you see, and I'm all alone here nights by myself. Being just a deputy, I couldn't take no responsibility along that line, not when I'm here by myself. You take this now—Drumwright might get his hands on you through the bars! He might kill you before I had any warning. I'm telling you, he's just that mean. So come back tomorrow. That is, if you still want to try to see him.

OCIE

Look here, brother! I've done thought this whole thing out. It wouldn't do me no good to come see him with them crowds hanging around out front. It's the nature of the gospel message that it reaches a man best when it's quiet and dark. Like now! In the night. Now's the time when he can look away deep down inside hisself and see hell a-burning there as plain as I see your very own face! And I don't have much time. You said so yourself, brother!

FATE

How in the world can I make you understand? Now fellow, that prisoner in yonder is . . . he's like a wild critter, a bobcat! I'm telling you facts. He ain't just any ordinary jailbird. You think he plays checkers or blows a French harp or gets somebody to write a post-card to his mama. Let me tell you, he don't. He just lays there, waiting! Preacher, what we got locked up

107

in yonder is *Buster Drumwright!* It's all you had to say in East Tennessee these past five years, just say the name, and it wasn't a man, woman, or boy didn't turn *pale.* I seen them get just as white around the mouth as a leghorn hen. Even now, when they come up here, I can see they're scared of him! Who wouldn't be? And now you're a preacher, and maybe Buster Drumwright is some sort of challenge to you. But he's a problem to me. You think I wouldn't rather be somewhere else right now than here? You might not understand this. Some preachers would, but you might not. I . . . well, I was courting a widow. Just found her in fact. Her husband was an older man, a railroader. He was driving this engine when she jumped the track coming out of Bristol. Smashed him dead. Left her young and all alone. She had nobody. See?

(*During this speech, the banjo offstage softly plunks eight bars of* I BEEN WORKING ON THE RAILROAD.)

OCIE

I understand, brother.

FATE

Like a speckled pup—she was pretty!—and we found one another! It was every man in this valley after her. (*The banjo is played.*)

And Isabel, she give herself—you know—to me. But then . . .

OCIE

Then what?

108

FATE

This all come up. We caught *him!* And it fell my job to stay here every dad-blasted night.

(*The sound of the banjo, played in a minor key*)

So, another man, he had her all to hisself, every night I couldn't go calling. And finally she sont me word. *Forget it,* that's what she said. And before that, she was all mine—all my own. *Forget it!*

OCIE

Lord have mercy! What sad news.

FATE

Yeah. And you think I didn't want to kick open that door yonder and blow Buster's dad-blasted head off! Damn the son of a bitch, anyway! I beg your pardon, Preacher. But I aimed to protect Isabel, to marry her —and now she's went bad and went to *whoring!* So it's problems all around, like the fellow says. But a man's duty is his duty. Life ain't some bed of rosebuds to lay up in. My place is here, Preacher, and I'm gonna see that bastard in yonder hanged legal, if it harelips this whole county! The way feelings is around here, I have to lock myself up in that jail just to take him his supper tray. And I never know what I'll find when I get back to this porch. Twice already they tried to jump me when I come out. Why, I ain't even taken his grub to him *yet.* That's how rough it's been tonight. I never had no chance.

OCIE

Give me the tray, brother.

109

(*Grabbing up the tray from the porch.*)
I'll take it to him. And while he eats I can talk to him about his salvation. Now that's a fair offer, ain't it? Well, ain't it?

FATE

All right. But I'll have to lock you in, understand. I hate to . . .

OCIE

I don't mind. I guess I'll have to have the key to his cell, won't I?

FATE

We don't unlock that cell door, Preacher. Not for no-body, not for no reason. Just slip his tray under the cell door.

OCIE

But how can I talk to him without I unlock his cell and go in to see him?

FATE

You talk to him through the bars. It's safer. Now you'll be extra careful, won't you, Preacher?

OCIE

I'll be extra careful.

(*Ocie goes in. The scrim wall fades. Buster lies asleep. Ocie raps on the bars to wake him.*)

BUSTER

Who the hell are you?

OCIE

I brought your supper.

BUSTER

About time! My belly's growling. Cold supper every

night! Everything covered with cold grease. Who are you, anyway?

OCIE

A preacher, I . . .

BUSTER

Well, get away from me, then. I don't have no use for preachers. You preachers! One was in here today trying to make me say I was sorry for what I done. Why should I be sorry? I got tomorrow and the next day. And then . . .

OCIE

Just let me say something . . .

BUSTER

Who are you, anyway? Some windbag. Hell, ain't I seen your kind before? Wanting to make a big show and go around telling folks how you converted Buster Drumwright. Yeah, that's it! That's a sapsucking preacher. Well, listen here, Preacher, you ain't converting me. I belong to the Devil! Yeah! And you can go to hell! SO GIT!

(*He hurls the tray at Ocie.*)

GET THIS PREACHER OUT OF HERE! GET HIM OUT, HEAR ME, STANHOPE! I'LL KILL HIM! YOU HEAR? HEAR ME, STANHOPE? Some preacher! Some bag of wind. You're just hot air, that's all. Go on. Git! That's the way! Git! Git to hell!

(*Ocie leaves, as Fate opens the door to let him out. The jail interior darkens.*)

FATE

I tried to tell you.

111

OCIE

I'll be back.

FATE

I tell you, Preacher, it's no use.
(*The stage dims out.*)

SCENE FOUR

[SETTING: The Hedgepath cabin. It is the same night. To indicate a time transition, the banjo theme is repeated once before the cabin is revealed.]
(*Ocie enters to find his brothers awaiting him. They spring up. Mary is asleep at the table, head in arms. She awakens but remains where she is. She shows a quiet relief when she discovers that Ocie has not killed Buster after all.*)

DAN

You got him! Did you, Ocie? What happened?

OCIE

I got inside the jail all right. Then . . .

DAN

And you nailed him! You just had to—you grabbed him, didn't you! Your hands . . .
(*He pauses, looks incredulous.*)
You didn't get him? Why? What got into you?

RANCE

Shut up, Dan! Let Ocie talk. Is there still any chance? Is there, Ocie?

112

OCIE

Listen now. There's still a chance. Now it's slim, but it's still a chance.

RANCE

Good, there's a chance. See?

DAN

You ain't went and gone yellow, have you, Ocie?

OCIE

Nobody's went yellow! I couldn't lay my hands on him. Stanhope let me in the jail, but he wouldn't let me in Buster's cell. It wasn't no chance to grab hold of him through the bars.

RANCE

Stanhope believed you was a preacher?

OCIE

He swallowed it hook, line, and sinker. He thinks I'm a genuine Bible-toting man of God, and he's going to let me in the jail tomorrow night, again. Now when I take Buster his supper tray, when I shove it under the door of his cell, why, it won't be no trick to slam him into the steel till I bash his brains out!

RANCE

But can't you get the key to his cell? Can't you slip it off Stanhope some way? What if you miss him grabbing through them bars? I don't like it, Ocie!

DAN

He's right, Ocie. We can't take no chances on you missing Buster Drumwright. You're the last chance we got. You . . . you just can't miss him! You can't!

OCIE

I asked Stanhope about getting into the cell. I asked

113

him first thing. But he said nothing doing. And I didn't get nowhere trying to convert Buster. When I says to him I'm a preacher, he cusses me.

DAN

I see the trouble now. You really been trying to *preach* to him.

OCIE

Well, I got to get him close up to those bars some way. How else would a preacher act if he didn't try to preach to him? He has to believe I'm a preacher.

RANCE

He's right. It's a better chance he can lay hands on him if he tries to convert him than if he tries grabbing at him through the bars. Just say he missed when he set down the supper tray. *Say he missed that first grab.* The show would be over then, because Buster would know what he was really up to, and we'd never get him.

DAN

I don't know. My mind's all worried. But if it don't work, we can still go down there, the three Hedgepath brothers, and shotgun or no shotgun, one of us can get through to Buster Drumwright. I just knew Ocie would get him tonight. But now, well! I'm turning in.

RANCE

Me too. Ain't you going to bed, Ocie?

OCIE

I got to study this Bible. I got to figure how to preach to him. What to say. It's got to be something good. I got to find some kind of bait in here to get his attention. To make him hungry, that's it!

114

(Dan and Rance climb to the loft. After they are gone, Mary raises her head.)

MARY

When I heard you come home, I was afraid you'd done it. I'm glad you didn't do it, Ocie. I keep hoping you'll give this idea up. It's blasphemy.

OCIE

I had no chance to do it.

MARY

I'm glad you didn't, Ocie. I got down on my knees and prayed.

OCIE

Queer woman, all balled up inside over a murderer.

MARY

Ocie, when you first come home, it give me hope you could set the boys straight. It give . . .

OCIE

So chickenhearted and soft. You can't help it, I guess. It's your way, your kind.

MARY

Ocie, all we had is trouble. You don't look like . . .

OCIE

Like a killer?

MARY

There's something kind about you. It has to be something kind in you.

OCIE

What you seen on me was the road, Mary. What you seen was all the places I been, the strange folks I seen, the things I knew along the way. What you seen was

115

what the road does to any man. Something soft and easy on the outside from knocking around the world and having no place, no home, no bed.

MARY

I knew I seen it. I knew you had to be different.

OCIE

But I'm home now. The road lays far behind me. And underneath what you see—underneath is all flint. So you may as well leave me be.

MARY

Ocie, I married into trouble. Ocie, if you won't listen to me, what will I do?

OCIE

Trouble? Lay down with it, woman. Live with it. I got just this night left to study. I got to find it tonight in here. Tomorrow night, when I go down there, I got to be smooth as a snake. I got to come up on his blind side, like silk.

MARY

Oh, *please.*

DAN (*From offstage*)

Get here, gal! Get to bed!

MARY

I'm coming, Dan! I prayed, at least, and I'm glad you didn't do it, Ocie. I prayed. I been praying.

OCIE

Get away! Go to bed and leave me be. I got to think! I got to study, I tell you!

MARY

Goodnight, Ocie.

116

DAN

Mary! What the hell you doing down there so long?
Get here!

(*Mary climbs to the loft. There is the noise of Dan slapping her.*)

MARY

You don't know how that hurts, Dan. You wouldn't
do it if you knew.

DAN

Shut your mouth!

(*The stage dims out.*)

SCENE FIVE

[SETTING: The jail. It is the following night. A noisy
crowd mills around.]

(*Ocie approaches studying the Bible. The crowd is
quieted at the Bystander's outburst.*)

BYSTANDER

Look yonder, boys! Studying that Bible mighty hard,
ain't you, Preacher?

OCIE

Everybody needs to study it. The whole world needs
to read this here book.

BYSTANDER

This must be the one you were talking about, Fate—
the one that wants to convert Buster Drumwright.

117

Well, you might just as well bat your head up against that stone wall yonder, Preacher. You'll never bring that heathen murderer to the Lord. Say, ain't I seen you before, Preacher?

OCIE

Maybe. I was by here last night.

BYSTANDER

So you was! Never would have suspected you for no preacher. I see it now, though. I ought to have figured you out the first time I seen you. It's sort of my hobby to figure strangers out. Stanhope, your preacher did come back, after all.

FATE

All right, Preacher. Come on. The rest of you stand back.

(*As the jail interior is lit, the outside goes dark.*)

BUSTER

You back, Preacher? I thought I run you off for good last night. Be damned if I ain't going to have to run you off all over again!

BYSTANDER

Hush your hollering that way at a man of God!

BUSTER

What's it to you, lardass, you sapsucking old tub of guts!

BYSTANDER

You'll go too far, Drumwright! The folks of this county have just about had all we're going to take off you and your wicked tongue!

WOMAN

And it's ladies present out here. Tell him that!

118

BUSTER

Tell that old sow of yours to hush squalling.

MOB

Let's get him! He's ours! We caught him! Give him over. Yah! What are we waiting for!

BUSTER

You're all yellow, that's what! Don't I wish I could bust out of here! Wouldn't I cut your damned hearts out and eat them!

BYSTANDER

Let's rush him!

FATE

The fair and legal hanging is day after tomorrow. You're all invited to be here at daylight.

BYSTANDER

Fair and legal. Ha! Treating *him* fair and legal—a dang heathen! How fair and legal was he, Stanhope, when he knifed the Hedgepath gal and her baby? Huh? What do we good folks owe a murdering wretch like him? Let us have him! We'll give him Christian justice all right! We'll let him have it right now! We'll put the fire to him!

WOMAN

Amen! Tell him, Fats! Amen!

MOB

Yeah!

FATE

You folks get on home! Get back away from here!

WOMAN

I never thought I'd see the time when a nice boy like you would protect a fiendish killer, Fate Stanhope!

119

FATE

Back, I say. Get going! Come on, Preacher.

BUSTER

That's the way! Get the hell on home! Just a bunch of damned stinking billy goats! No guts in the lot! No guts! You hear?

FATE

Shut up, Buster!

(*The mob is gone as Buster leaves the window. Fate lets Ocie into the jail and locks the security door after him. The scrim wall fades as Ocie confronts Buster again, stooping to push the supper tray under his cell door.*)

OCIE

Here's your supper. This time it's hot.

BUSTER

Push it all the way—all the way under, Preacher. That's the time! So you really come back. I never seen much grit in a preacher before. Where'd you get all that grit from, Preacher?

OCIE

I have something to tell you. I got good news for you.

BUSTER

For me? Good news? Ain't that a joke! You ought to be in the vaudeville, Preacher! Missed your calling, that's what.

OCIE

Just because you're in jail, that's no cause to give up hope.

BUSTER

Who the hell says I give up hope? Huh? I'm going to

120

bust out of this tin can. No jail can hold Buster!

OCIE

Well, what if you don't bust out, though? What then?

BUSTER

They'll just hang me day after tomorrow, that's all.
What you *think* they'll do?

OCIE

All right! But after you're dead. Where will you be
then? Say they've done put the noose to your neck and
sprung the trap. Where are you now?

BUSTER

Good God! Just like every last one of them sapsucking
preachers, ain't you, fellow? Always talking about hell
and damnation! The fire and the brimstone! Well now,
fellow, I'm going there. Don't you see? It won't do you
no good at all *telling* me about hell, because I'm going
to find out everything there is to know about that place
in a couple of days from now—if I don't bust out of this
trap. So you just save your sapsucking wind. Hell-talk!
Hell, hell, hell! That's all you know to tell a fellow
about. And you come sneaking in here talking about
good news. Ain't that a good one?

OCIE

Well now, did you ever hear of St. Paul?

BUSTER

Paul? Ain't he in the Bible? Sure I heard of him. Who
ain't, I'd like to know! It's people named after him
walking around today.

(*He pauses.*)

Fact, I had a friend once named Paul. He was running
off some moonshine whiskey at our still, and this

121

revenue agent shot him right through the head. I was right beside of him when he fell, and I looked down beside me there—and Paul was dead, and his eyes was still wide open, like yours. I grabbed my rifle and fell down rolling. I rolled sideways, over and over, about fifty steps, before I started shooting. I killed three of them sapsuckers, and the fourth one, he run off before I could get a bead on him. Preacher, that last son of a bitch caught air! Busted through vines and tree limbs, jumped the creek, waded the briers. Run just like a hill rabbit, dropped his hat and his pistol! I had to lay down and laugh at the way that peckerwood run. Like a scared horse! But then . . . and then, you know, I went back over to where Paul was laying, and . . . and I knew it wasn't Paul no more. It was something . . . something else I had not ever saw before, till right then. What was it you was saying?

OCIE

I was saying about Paul. He was in jail plenty of times. They picked him up on vagrancy and throwed him in the drunk tank. They beat the whey out of him plenty of times and made him lay down and sleep on the floor where the drunks puked.

BUSTER

Don't kid me, fellow. How could they put a saint in jail? Don't try pulling my leg, Preacher, because if it's one thing I know it's this—nobody in the Bible was ever in jail. Not Paul anyway. Not a good guy like him.

122

OCIE

No, it's true, sure enough. Paul hoboed and bummed around. Hopped freights, maybe. Or if he found a peach tree and he was hungry, maybe he plucked his-self a snack of fruit. He didn't do nothing really bad, you know. But every now and so often, they still got him on vagrancy. Why, once they had him in this prison at this town, and the Lord sent down an earth-quake. It shaken things so hard it busted open the cell doors, and Paul and his buddies just walked out, big as you please. Paul even had the Mayor and the Board of Aldermen come up and apologize for locking him up in the first place! It's the kind of fellow Paul was. He was a real man! He never give up hope. No, sir!

BUSTER

I . . . I just can't hardly believe there could be nothing like that in the Bible. Nobody never said anything about it to me before. It's kind of hard to believe.

OCIE

Listen, friend. I just got through reading it *last night*. Yes I did, it's in this very book, all about him. And that's the good news.

BUSTER

There you go. Preaching again! Trying to trick me with all that stuff about Paul. Paul wouldn't use no tricks! He wouldn't have to.

OCIE

Well, Paul was a preacher. He preached the good news. That was his trade.

123

BUSTER

Well now, I never thought of that—that Paul was a preacher. You wonder why a good man like him would want to preach. You wonder. Now just for fun . . . (*He hesitates.*)

. . . I mean, now what would I have to do to be saved, Preacher? Not that I'd ever do it. Don't get me wrong.

OCIE

Oh, it's easy. Just repent your sins, is all. Then you confess Christ as your Saviour, and you're baptized.

BUSTER

Baptized?

OCIE

It's where they stick you down under the water and wash all your . . .

BUSTER

Sure, I know. I heard of being baptized before. But I never was, of course. And I never will be. How could you baptize anybody through this? What a joke!

OCIE

If you was really interested in getting baptized, I could ask. I could see about it and . . .

BUSTER

Forget it, Preacher. Maybe I just went soft for a minute there. It was a crazy idea. What ever happened to him, anyway?

OCIE

What happened? To who?

124

BUSTER

To Paul. What ever become of him?

OCIE

Oh, why he went on preaching. They even converted this jailer once and . . .

BUSTER

I'm talking about the end. How did Paul die? What happened to him?

OCIE

What makes you so all-fired interested in that, all of a sudden? Ain't . . . ain't how he *lived* the important thing? Ain't *that* more important?

BUSTER

Naw, Preacher. Not to me, it ain't.

OCIE

Well, look. I got to be leaving.

BUSTER

I might have knew you would! And you ain't coming back either, are you, Preacher? Giving me up, ain't you? Well, you might as well give me up, because nobody's converting Buster Drumwright. See what I mean? Nobody!

OCIE

Now look, I got to go. But I promise to be back here tomorrow night. I'll tell you what happened to him, to Paul—tomorrow, all right?

BUSTER

Why not now? Any preacher ought to know that. Well, shouldn't he? Don't you know?

125

OCIE

Hell yes . . . I mean, sure I do! But it's a real long story. You can't tell it in two words, not about somebody as important as Paul. Anyway, you ain't interested in getting baptized, so what's the use?

BUSTER

I never said I wasn't *interested,* did I?

OCIE

Now say . . . say something could be figured out—if it could be fixed some way—would you be baptized?

BUSTER

I . . . well, I don't know.

OCIE

Look, you ain't got much time! It's only tomorrow night left, and then . . .

BUSTER

The rope. I know it. Well . . .

OCIE

Well, how about it now?

BUSTER

Put it this way. If . . . if you can fix it up, then I might. But now I ain't saying I will!

OCIE

But you might.

BUSTER

Anyway, you can tell me the rest about Paul, how he died. Then I'll decide—that is, if you can fix it up with the deputy.

OCIE

I'll tell you about Paul next time. Right now I got to go, I got to leave.

126

BUSTER

You're giving me up, ain't you?

OCIE

Look, fellow, I ain't giving you up. You got to believe it! But like I tried to explain to you nice, I got other things—something else to do right now.

BUSTER

See you tomorrow night then, Preacher.

OCIE

Yeah.

(*Ocie raps on the security door as the jail interior fades out. Fate unlocks the door, and Ocie comes out.*)

FATE

Leaving, Preacher?

OCIE

It's awful rough, a mighty rough thing.

FATE

I tried to tell you, Preacher. Others tried it before. They all failed on him.

OCIE

Maybe you don't understand. I'm going to convert him, Deputy.

FATE

Him? You mean you're getting somewhere?

OCIE

That's it. I seen it happen too many times before, not to know the signs. He's a-teetering on the very edge of salvation. It's how he breathes, the way his eyes look at you. His hands tremble a little bit. But . . .

FATE

What's bothering you?

127

OCIE

Well, say he does confess Christ tomorrow night, like I'm sure he will. Say I bring him to the Lord on his knees, and he sees the glory of heaven before his eyes. Say he repents and wants to embrace Jesus Christ. It ain't no way in the world I know of that I can baptize him. I hate to have to face him with that part, to cut him off from the Lord just when . . . when he's ready to fall in my hands like a ripe peach.

FATE

Do you have to baptize him, Preacher?

OCIE

If he ain't baptized, he ain't saved, brother! If he ain't baptized, we all been wasting our time.

FATE

That's a tough one, all right. I mean, I ain't got much feeling about him, but if he called on the Lord . . .

OCIE

It's what I'm trying to tell you, brother! He's going to do it! And now look—say if I was to get a tub somewhere, and we was to set it in yonder before his cell, tomorrow night . . .

FATE

Couldn't you just throw some water at him through the bars? Maybe you could talk to my uncle—now he's full of ideas.

OCIE

Now look, brother. In the first place, a man can't receive the Lord through prison bars. You can't throw the Lord through them bars. My hands have to be

128

laid upon him, and he has to be pushed down under the water to cleanse him! And now what if I went to your uncle? What if I went to him and folks started yelling and carrying on about they didn't want Buster Drumwright to be baptized. What if your uncle told me no?

FATE

He might at that. A sheriff has got to be a politician.

OCIE

Course he has, brother! So we set up the tub in yonder, and you give me the key. You lock me up in yonder, so I can bring him out and baptize him. It's up to you.

FATE

Naw, I just can't, I . . .

OCIE

Hold on a second. You going to stand between another man and his salvation? Is that something you want on your heart the rest of your livelong days—that you let him walk up them new pine steps on that new scaffold yonder, that you stood by close and smelled that new lumber and let him step out on the trap door, hands bound behind him, and let him drop down into eternal hell-fire? You better think a minute!

(*He hands the Bible to Fate and leads him to contemplate the gallows tree.*)

FATE

I . . . I guess you're right, Preacher. I couldn't stand between no man and his salvation! A politician could. Yeah, a politician could in a minute. But then I ain't

129

no politician, not yet, anyway. So maybe I won't never be sheriff of this county like I planned to some day. Naw, Preacher, I wouldn't stand in the way of a man and his salvation, if you was to offer me the whole great state of Tennessee with a new fence built around it. You get a tub, Preacher.

(*He hands the Bible back to Ocie.*)

OCIE

God will reward you for this, Deputy. I better say good-night.

FATE

Just bring a tub! Because you got to live with yourself forever. Because you couldn't block him off from his salvation—no matter who the son of a bitch is, nor what he done—not and live with yourself after that!

[THE END OF ACT ONE]

Act Two

SCENE ONE

[SETTING: The interior of the Hedgepath cabin. It is the same night.]

(*Dan sits on the bench beside the fireplace, whittling. Suddenly he begins to stab the knife repeatedly into the wood of the bench.*)

DAN

I'm sick and tired of waiting, of wondering every minute, has he done it or not!

RANCE

Don't fly off the handle!

MARY

Your conscience is bothering you, Dan.

DAN

You shut up!

(*Ocie enters, breathless.*)

RANCE

Ocie!

OCIE

I got out of sight, and then I lit out running.

RANCE

We'll hide you. They'll never find you . . .

DAN

So you got him, after all!

MARY

Ocie, no!

DAN

Ain't I warned you to keep your mouth shut? Am I going to have to wring your neck?

OCIE

Leave her be! Leave her be and listen.

RANCE

So you finally got him!

OCIE

No, I ain't got him yet. But listen—wait now! I found the *way* to get him. I tell you, it might just work.

RANCE

Hear that, Dan? He's found a way. It's going to work!

DAN

When you come in so fast and flustered, I thought you had done got him. I thought this waiting was finally over. It's getting me down—no sleep at night, minding them bobbins at that sapsucking mill all day—thinking tonight we'll get him! I can't stand it much longer!

OCIE

It's nearly all fixed up. It hit me all of a sudden tonight, when Buster asked me about getting baptized.

MARY

Baptized. You mean you're really converting him, Ocie?

DAN

No, he ain't converting him. For the last time, Ocie's trying to kill him. He's going to kill him.

132

RANCE

Go on, what happened?

OCIE

Well, it busted all over me like thunder—that if I could get my hands on him to baptized him, then I could . . .

RANCE

Sure, you could strangle him like we planned.

OCIE

Better than that. I could push him down under the water, down all the way under, and just hold him there.

DAN

You're going to do it! I knowed all along you could. You're going to get him!

OCIE

So I got out of there fast as I could, and when I told Fate Stanhope that Buster was wanting to be baptized you should have seen his jaw slack. He looked like he'd been mauled over the head.

DAN

You had him there. I can just see it. How could he say no? He couldn't.

RANCE

What did he say?

OCIE

It's like Dan says, what could he say? Couldn't no man stand in the way of another's salvation, could he? So he thought a minute . . .

133

DAN

Just tell us what he said, Ocie!

OCIE

He said all right, I could take Buster Drumwright out of the cell tomorrow night and baptize him. Just get a tub.

DAN

I knowed it! I been praying you'd find a way to get him, Ocie.

OCIE

It's just this one hitch.

RANCE

A hitch?

OCIE

Yeah. Buster ain't said for certain if he will be baptized or not.

DAN

But you just said he would.

OCIE

I said he was interested. I need . . . I need to know some Bible stuff. I need . . .

DAN

Get over here, Mary, and listen here to what Ocie needs.

OCIE

I need to know what ever become of Paul. That's what I need first—how he died.

DAN

Well, how did Paul die? Tell him, Mary!

134

MARY

He was martyred. The Bible don't say, but they think
he was killed at Rome.

OCIE

But how did they kill him?

DAN

How did Paul die? Tell him, Mary!

MARY

I imagine the lions tore him apart. I guess . . . I don't
know. They used to throw them to the lions.

OCIE

That's good enough. I'll improve on that a little bit.
Buster ought to go for it.

DAN

He will, he'll fall for it like a chicken on a June bug.
Lions! I kind of like it myself!

RANCE

What else you need to know?

OCIE

Well. I need some scripture to read to him, something
to melt his heart like . . . well, something to make him
feel like crying.

DAN

All right, woman, you heard him. Find Brother Ocie
some scripture like that. You always got your nose
pushed down in this book.

MARY

I . . .
(*She is frightened and confused.*)

135

DAN

Find it, I said. I'll give you about one minute!

MARY

I like the third chapter of Colossians.

OCIE

Wait a minute! Did Paul write it?

MARY

Yes.

DAN

All right, let's hear it.

MARY

(*She reads with great feeling.*)

"If ye then be risen with Christ, seek those things which are above, where Christ sitteth on the right hand of God. Set your affection on things above, not on things on the earth. For ye are dead, and your life is hid with Christ in God. When Christ, who is our life, shall appear, then shall ye also appear with him in glory."

(*There is a silence.*)

DAN

That's enough.

RANCE

What you think, Ocie?

OCIE

He's mighty near to death. He's so near to dying, in fact, it ought to get him.

DAN

It will! Hell-fire, it'll get him. It damned near got me. He'll bawl like a baby. Mark the place, Mary.

136

OCIE

I'll mark it myself.

(*He takes the Bible from Mary.*)

"When Christ, who is our life, shall appear, then shall ye also appear with him in glory." I'd have to call that a mighty big order for Buster Drumwright. Can you see *him* in glory?

RANCE

Naw, but I can see him in hell. And you're fixing to send him there, Ocie. Ever think about that?

OCIE

Not if he's baptized! I'm sending Mr. Buster H. Drumwright to heaven, remember?

RANCE

Be dang if you ain't! It's so . . . so pretty. It's like a smooth-operating machine. It's about the prettiest thing I ever seen, for a fact. You kill two birds with one stone, all in one little smooth operation, just by holding a fellow under the water a little bit longer. Well, you need anything else?

OCIE

I got to get a bathtub somewhere and get it hauled up to the jail. We'll set it up in the hall outside his cell and . . .

DAN

A bathtub?

OCIE

It's got to be something big, and it's got to be nice. I figure a nice big bathtub . . .

137

RANCE

How about a barrel? Wouldn't be no trouble to get a barrel. But now a *bathtub* . . .

OCIE

You can't drown no man in a barrel! It would flop over. Listen, I done thought it out. Down in Dallas I had this . . . this lady friend . . . and she lived in a house where they had a bathtub. It had iron feet on it, like lion's paws, and it was hooked up to hot and cold running tap water. Why, you couldn't have turned that son of a bitch over with . . . with a brace of mules! And it was white—just as pure and white as snow. Hell, I seen several, none nice as hers—Imogene's— but it's what we got to have now. You just can't tempt no man hard as Buster Drumwright is to let hisself be baptized in just anything!

RANCE

Ocie, you ain't in Dallas. This is Trammel County, Tennessee.

OCIE

Huh?

DAN

He means to say that bathtubs like that don't just grow on every bush in . . . in Trammel County.

RANCE

Was there any bathtubs like that around here when you left and run off?

OCIE

Naw, but I been gone a long time. Electric lights has

come in. I didn't expect to find no tub like that here at home—but somewhere! You mean we can't get no nice tub?

DAN

I got the trough I used to dip sheep in . . .

RANCE

Naw, we can't take no chances. It is one new bathtub in town—Mr. Turner's. I heard 'em talking about it up at the mill. It's about what you was telling you saw in Dallas—maybe not as big as all that, but it's got feet and all.

DAN

We'd have to unhook it. I don't know as he'd let us borrow anything like that—proud of it as they are.

OCIE

Well, it's what I need. It has to be something so nice that Buster will just have to say yes.

RANCE

I just remembered.

DAN

What?

RANCE

Mr. Turner's took his family out of town. We can borrow his tub, I guess.

DAN

So he has. I knowed that peckerwood was a coward, but when he left so his family couldn't watch the hanging. . . . That's the kind of man we got for superintendent up at the mill. Well, I never unhooked a bathtub,

139

but it's got to be a first time for everything, eh, boys?

RANCE

We'll get the tub some way. We'll get it up to the jail.

OCIE

It's all in the world I need now.

DAN

And when you take him out, you'll be thinking about Kathleen and her little child! You'll have the steel in your hands to wipe this stain off the name of Hedge-path. You'll push him down under that water . . . and then . . . when you don't pull him out . . . he'll have time . . . to think about the ones he killed, before his breath gives out. Before his wind dies on him, he'll know it's a revenger has got him! And he'll commence to suck water . . . and the air . . . the air's going to bubble out of him. Oh, Ocie, I wish it was me doing it in the place of you!

OCIE

I'll be thinking about you, Dan.

RANCE

And me, think of me too.

OCIE

All right, Rance—you too.

DAN

I dreamed last night—dreamed you done it, Ocie. It felt so good when the news come that Buster Drumwright was dead. It was like . . . like Christmastime back a long time ago when we was kids, when Maw and Dad and Kathleen was still living. I'll be so glad when I can wake up every morning and know Kath-

140

leen's death is avenged. I guess I been fearing it would fail. But now . . .

OCIE

I won't fail. Once I get him in that tub, I'll have him! When you going to show me where Kathleen and her baby's buried?

DAN

After you've killed Buster, I'll take you there. It's a right pretty spot, all green and grassy and nice, and it's a redbud tree growing nearby. Kathleen loved the sight of redbuds blooming, bees muzzling the blossoms—I figured it was the right place for her to lie.

OCIE

She did love the springtime. Living, being alive was such . . . a pleasure to Kathleen.

RANCE

Can't you see how she used to pluck flowers and pin them to her bonnet and Maw's before we set out for church? First you, Ocie, you run away, then the old folks died . . . and Kathleen married and moved out . . . and now this . . . it's mighty near killed us, Ocie! Too hard, too awful.

OCIE

I better sleep. I'll need all my strength tomorrow evening.

(Rance and Dan go wearily into the loft, leaving Ocie and Mary.)

MARY

Were you warm enough last night, Ocie? Your bed all right?

141

OCIE

My bed's fine.

(*He fetches his pallet from beside the fireplace.*)

MARY

Would Kathleen want you to do this thing, Ocie? I knew her too, Ocie. I loved her too.

OCIE

Lay off! This ain't none of your business. You never loved her, to say such a thing! A wrong is something you got to avenge, woman!

MARY

But I did, I did love her, Ocie. She wouldn't want you to kill him.

(*Ocie rolls out his pallet on the floor beside the table.*)

OCIE

Leave me be!

MARY

Ocie, won't you listen?

OCIE

Get on! Get away! Let me lay down in peace!

MARY (*Wearily*)

Good night, Ocie.

(*She climbs into the loft. Ocie has lain down. Now he gets up, fetches the Bible and a lamp, puts the oil lamp on the floor at the head of his pallet, and lies down to read. The stage dims out.*)

142

SCENE TWO

[Setting: The Hedgepath cabin at the next day's end. To indicate a time transition, the banjo theme is repeated before the cabin is revealed. Sunset is seen burning beyond the windows. Night slowly falls as this scene progresses.]

(*Dan and Rance enter. Mary is stooped before the fireplace, cooking. Ocie lies asleep on the pallet.*)

DAN

He been asleep all this time?

MARY

Like a dead man.

RANCE

I guess he sat up nearly all night studying that Bible. I come down just before dawn, and there he laid, with the book open, still reading, wide awake.

DAN

Let's wake him. He'll be glad to hear we got the tub.

RANCE

Let him sleep while he can! I don't want to think about that tub. I never felt so wrong about doing a thing in my life. Busting in another man's house and cutting his prize, his brand-new tub away from the pipes . . .

DAN

Wouldn't have been so bad if we could have shut the water off first, Rance. Sawing them pipes in the face of all that water was the worst, and then you had to drop your end coming down the stairs.

RANCE

My foot slipped.

143

DAN

For a minute, I thought that big white son of a bitch was going to run over me and bust my back! What if I couldn't have held it?

RANCE

Stealing a man's tub. It was hateful.

MARY

Is that all that bothers you? Taking a tub, is that all you think you're doing?

RANCE

I never bargained for no stealing! I just never bargained for it!

MARY

But you bargained for killing. You bargained for blasphemy.

DAN

That's right, Rance. Hell, taking a tub don't make no difference! We had to have it! Even Mary can see the sense of that.

RANCE

I bargained for killing Buster Drumwright, that's all.

OCIE (*Waking*)

So you got the tub. That's good.

DAN

We hid it back of the jail. Buster was putting on a show around in front, and we just come in behind and hid it in the weeds. It's a real booger, Ocie! Damned if it won't weigh almost a ton. It's got feet just like you wanted.

RANCE

It was a bad thing, Ocie. It was in a special room all

144

to itself upstairs, sitting there all quiet and still and white . . . as cotton. We sawed the pipes, and water went spouting everwhere. Well, your tub's down there, Ocie.

OCIE

We had to have something nice or else . . .

PREACHER

Hello!

OCIE!

Who the hell is that?

MARY

The Preacher's here.

RANCE

Run him off! Damn him, anyway—always meddling!

OCIE

Just get rid of him!

(*He goes into the loft.*)

MARY

Preacher . . .

PREACHER

I had tidings this afternoon, bad tidings from Knox County, and I said, I better look in and pray with the Hedgepaths! Praise God! I better take them the awful news!

MARY

News?

PREACHER

Knowing how you feel, how hard on you it was, admiring how you've stayed away from it all this time and never once mixed up in it yourselves. Even with all the hatred against Buster Drumwright in the air.

145

I said, Dan and Rance would want to know what they've kept out of. Maybe I come at a bad time, I don't know.

RANCE

MARY

You're always welcome in this house, Preacher.

RANCE

Sure, Preacher.

DAN

You brung news about Drumwright?

PREACHER

The worst kind. A bunch from Knox County is on the way here to join forces with our bunch. There'll be no earthly way to stop that big a crowd from taking Buster Drumwright out and burning him alive. I appealed to the sheriff to call in help. I begged him on bended knees, and all he did was to send word to Fate Stanhope—to tell Fate that if that many rushes him, it'll be best to turn over the keys and let them have Drumwright. So I said, well, you might as well tear that gallows down and burn the courthouse for all the law means in this county. You know what he said to me then—to me, a prophet of religion?

DAN

What did he say?

PREACHER

He said, "I'm keeping my nose out of it, Preacher, and you better do the same."

RANCE

This bunch from Knoxville. When will they get here?

146

PREACHER

I wouldn't be surprised if they ain't already there by now. They left Knoxville about three this afternoon.

DAN

What are we going to do?

RANCE

I knowed it! The minute we laid a hand to that tub, I tell you! Now look what's happened!

PREACHER

I never expected it to upset you this much, boys. I come to have prayer.

MARY

Preacher, they're plotting to kill Buster—Dan and Rance and Ocie!

DAN

Mary!

(*Ocie comes down from the loft.*)

PREACHER

I don't understand. I come to have prayer. Who is this?

MARY

This is Ocie. He's pretending to be a preacher to get in the jail and kill Buster.

PREACHER

Ocie? But we thought you . . . maybe you was dead—the years you been away.

DAN

He come back.

RANCE

Yeah, Preacher. Ocie come home.

147

PREACHER

Then you're the man they mean, the one that's gone down in the dead of night, trying to save Buster Drumwright's soul. Who would have guessed any man would dare to blaspheme in that way? I'll have to warn Fate Stanhope.

(*The brothers grab the Preacher. Rance holds a gun on him. Dan opens his knife.*)

MARY

Dan!

PREACHER

It's all right, Mary!

MARY

They don't know what they're doing, Preacher. They've gone crazy.

PREACHER

"Unto thee, O Lord, do I lift up my soul. O my God, I trust in thee: let me not be ashamed, let not mine enemies triumph over me. Yea, let none that wait on thee be ashamed . . ."

RANCE

Shut up, you bastard! Hush, or by God, I'll kill you!

PREACHER

No offense, Rance. I already said I know how you feel. I know how you loved Kathleen. I know your brothers' love for that babe. These hills . . . these hills are my home too, ain't they?

DAN

He's got a sight more sense on it than Mary, by God!

148

MARY

They ain't thinking about Kathleen, Preacher. All they can think of is vengeance! When Ocie come home, I had such high hopes.

PREACHER

The Lord said, "Vengeance is mine."

RANCE

An eye for an eye, Preacher. A tooth for a tooth.

MARY

You don't believe that. None of you believe that. You're good men at heart. The spirit of Christ is in you, but you're denying him.

DAN

Wait and see if we don't believe it. Hear me, woman?

OCIE

You and your Bible-talk. Trying to talk us out of what we must do. We had a terrible thing happen to our family, and if you had any backbone, if you was really a member of this family . . .

MARY

I am in this family.

OCIE

If you was really a Hedgepath, then you'd see. You'd hush your mousy talking!

PREACHER

Maybe you better hush, Mary.

MARY

Stand by silent and see them do this thing? Not and call myself a Christian, I can't. Preacher, talk them out of

149

it. I've been praying, like you said, praying Ocie wouldn't do it. Preacher, they're going to hang Buster Drumwright, anyway.

DAN

Or burn him! We got to do something, Ocie. We can't let them get him first!

MARY

No, Dan, please. Ocie, think what you're about to do!

PREACHER

Yes, he better think.

OCIE

They don't understand. The Bible's made them blind. But if it was their sister, they'd be singing a different tune. They'd be so mad they'd want to go down there and kill him theirselves. They'd see red just like we do.

MARY

Ocie, tell them you won't go.

OCIE

Betray my own brothers? Go back on them now? Listen, I left out from here when I was thirteen years old, and after then, I never hit a lick to support this family. Paw was dead. And I never even come home to see my own maw buried.

MARY

Ocie, God gave his only son. We're Christians, Ocie—Christians.

OCIE

Never knew my own maw was dead. My sis marries some no-count ridgerunner, still no Ocie. Off roaming

150

the world! They could starve to death for all I knowed.
If I'd just stayed home and worked, maybe it wouldn't
none of it have happened. But I was a dern bum—a
drifter. No better than Ralph Swiggert!

MARY

Killing Buster Drumwright ain't going to help. It'll
destroy us. It'll only wipe out what few Hedgepaths
are left. They'll run us out of the county. We'll be
scattered like the leaves in wintertime, Ocie.

OCIE

That's a lie. They'll thank us. They'll thank me. They'll
say Ocie Hedgepath finally come home and took over
his family responsibilities. Ocie Hedgepath—they'll
point at me—he defended his family's pride. I'll be
what I never been, not once in my whole life before
this here night coming on—I'll be a hero.

MARY

You're all thinking crazy. What can be inside you, I
wonder, to make you think that way?

OCIE

You don't think it, woman! You feel it. It burns deep
down like hot ashes in your chest, and you lay awake
at night, burning all over. You lay there, and you
listen to what's pumping in your veins. It's your blood
and kin, and if you're a Hedgepath, you feel it—you
know! Naw, you ain't one of us!

MARY

Such a dread and chill is on my heart. I wonder if God
put some curse on us, Preacher? Can't you make Ocie

151

see what he's fixing to do? Ocie . . . Ocie, don't you see the end . . . the end of everything?

OCIE

I got to think! Say the wrong thing down yonder tonight, and maybe I won't get my hands on him. Make a wrong move, and something might be wrong. He might get away from me. He might holler.

MARY

Kill Buster Drumwright, and right then, you kill this family too. There won't be no family left!

DAN

That's who he is thinking about.

RANCE

Ocie's right. We got to play safe. We got to make sure.

PREACHER

Don't you boys get me wrong. I see your side of it.

RANCE

You do? Ain't that nice of you!

DAN

We got to do something! We got to move!

OCIE

You and Rance better bring the Preacher to the jail with you. I'll run on ahead. They might get to Buster before I do.

PREACHER

He's right. Ocie's right, boys. Stanhope's nerves are shot. That kid's been sitting out there all night, week after week. If that big bunch rushes him, he'll hand over the keys. He'll have to!

152

RANCE

All right. We'll bring the Preacher with us. Preacher, now don't try nothing.

PREACHER

I see it *your* way, boys! Never *knew* before this how strong you felt about it. See what I mean? Never entered my head.

DAN

Then you won't mind if I have to hold a knife on you, will you, Preacher? You don't care if I keep my eye on you a little?

PREACHER

Not a bit, Dan. Listen, ain't I lived hereabouts all my life? Don't I know how a man's feeling runs at a time like this?

RANCE

What about Mary?

OCIE

Leave her here.

MARY

Go on, Rance. Shoot me! That's what you're thinking. Ain't it? You might as well. We've all found our destruction.

OCIE

Let's go. Now you boys hold back and keep out of it. Don't say nothing.

(*Ocie leaves.*)

MARY

Making a murderer, a blasphemer, of your own

153

brother! Sending him ahead to be killed and damned! You were never Christians—none of you. Fetch him back, Dan. Go fetch him back! Dan, please!

DAN

All right, Preacher. Let's go.

PREACHER

I'm with you. Praise God! Shall we first kneel in prayer?

MARY

Prayer!

DAN

Now God damn it, woman, kneel! Can't you see we're in a hurry?

(*They all kneel, with the exception of Rance.*)

RANCE

Maybe I'll just bow my head, if it's all right with you, Preacher.

(*He closes in on the Preacher with the rifle.*)

PREACHER

Why *sure,* Rance! That's *all right* this time, I guess! (*He begins the prayer.*)

O great merciful God, look down with pity and compassion on thy servant Mary Hedgepath. These are . . . are troublesome days for Mary, Lord. O Lord, help her to understand what these brothers must do. Guide her through this life, and bring her to salvation in the end. In the name of Jesus Christ. Amen.

(*Dan, Rance, and the Preacher leave. Mary runs out, following them into the darkness.*)

154

MARY

Dan? Dan?

SCENE THREE

[SETTING: The jail, the same night. Torchlight flickering from off stage right adds to a sense of heat and of impending violence.]

(*A howling mob stands before the jail, while Fate Stanhope, two steps above them on the porch, holds them at bay with his gun. They quiet down as the Bystander speaks. Buster is at the window.*)

BYSTANDER

You may as well give us the keys, Fate. There are too many of us now.

FATE

I'd hate to have to shoot you. I'd hate it bad, to have to shoot any of you. Now put them torches away. Put them out and go on back home!

BYSTANDER

Don't make us burn the jail to get him, Fate. The keys —hand us the keys.

MOB

Burn the jail! Let's burn it down!

BUSTER

Don't worry, Fate. I wouldn't blame you if you gave over the keys.

155

FATE

What the hell's come over you? So you finally got the fear of God put in you, huh? Afraid, eh? The great Buster Drumwright, the mad-dog killer.

BUSTER

Think what you please. I just said I wouldn't blame you none if you let them take me.

FATE

Well, I ain't going to give them the satisfaction, nor you, neither. I'm going to see that rope tied on your neck good and legal.

BYSTANDER

Well, do you give us the keys, or do we have to take them off of you? Which is it going to be?

OCIE

Can I say something?
(*He shoves his way through the crowd and mounts to the porch.*)

FATE

It won't do no good, Preacher.

BYSTANDER

You're too late, Preacher! We've made up our minds!

OCIE

If you can just give me a minute . . .

BYSTANDER

You can have a minute, Preacher. Hey, let the preacher have his say. What are you—heathens?

MOB

All right! All right, Preacher! Let him have his *say*— sure!

156

OCIE

Maybe . . . maybe it's something you fellows don't understand. Now I know how you feel about this man. But now, I also know some things about him you don't know. Because you see . . . you see I come all the way here from Dallas, Texas, just to try to save his soul. Friends, I walked the greatest part of that distance. I come over rocks and sand. The sun scorched me during the day. The sweat run down in my eyes. Nights, I shivered with nothing but this old coat to cover me. Holes wore in these shoes, and I cut cardboard and bottomed them. I come through all that and more I could tell. I come all that way just to bring probably the worst sinner in the world to Jesus Christ. But . . . but, my friends, I wanted this man to have the good news before ever he died. God brought me down tonight, my friends.

BYSTANDER

That's right. This preacher come all the way from Texas, from way out West.

OCIE

I come down here tonight—it being the last night Buster Drumwright will be alive on this earth . . .

WOMAN

You're right there, Preacher!

MOB

You can say that again. Yeah! Yeah!

OCIE

I come down here tonight for the last time, in order to baptize him. Ain't that right, Deputy?

157

FATE

It's the gospel truth. It sure is. He's the only preacher that never give up. The rest tried and failed. But this man kept a-coming. He's telling the truth.

OCIE

I can't baptize him after he's dead, can I? I ain't asking no favor for myself. All I'm asking you to do is grant God a favor. I'm asking you to give me a little time to bring this man to Christ. And now . . . now I ain't trying to turn you from your purpose. For I ain't nothing but a poor preacher. Just another fellow without a dime to his name and no place to lay his head at night. I ain't trying to turn you from your purpose, because I couldn't do it noways, no matter how hard I tried. But folks, I come a long way to do this work.

FATE

How about it, boys?

BYSTANDER

Let's give the preacher a chance. I know I don't aim to interfere with the Lord. Don't none of us aim to do that.

(*He removes his hat.*)

OCIE

It's a bathtub around back of the jail there. Can some of you bring it around here?

FATE

Sure, Preacher.

BYSTANDER

Come on, let's get that tub!

(*Several members of the crowd bear the bathtub in.*)

158

MAN

A few strong backs—that's all it takes, fellows!

MOB

Here we go! Bring her along easy!

WOMAN

My, ain't it a nice tub though! Careful, boys!

OCIE

If you'll let me in, I'll get him ready.

FATE

You just worked a miracle, Preacher. Two minutes ago they was ready to lynch him.

(*Fate opens the security door. The jail interior lights up as the procession enters.*)

MAN

Don't drop her, boys! Easy does it now! Let her down slow!

(*The tub is set up in the jail outside Buster's cell. Men enter through the security door, bringing buckets of water. Ocie drags a stool close to the bars in order to talk to Buster. Throughout the events leading up to the baptism the sound of the tub being filled forms a background against which the conversation between Buster and Ocie is pitched. At first the buckets come rapidly. But towards the end they are spaced farther and farther apart, so that both men unconsciously begin to listen for the sound of water being poured into the tub, as the action nears its close.*)

BUSTER

You come back. You come, and I knowed you was coming, Preacher.

159

OCIE

I never had no chance to ask if you had decided to be baptized or not.

(*He pauses as water is poured.*)

Happens that way sometimes.

(*Water is poured.*)

I had to act sort of quick out yonder.

(*Water is poured.*)

BUSTER

It taken guts to stand up in front of a bunch like that and beg for me. You . . . you ain't just no ordinary preacher. They might have shot you down, and you knowed they might do it. Still, you did it. Why, I've killed many a man for less than that. It's how I know that what you done . . .

(*Water is poured.*)

. . . taken guts.

OCIE

Oh, I had plenty to gain by it, is why I done it.

(*Water is poured.*)

You got Christ in your heart, and the chance of death don't mean nothing. A man don't have to think. He just jumps in and . . .

(*Water is poured.*)

You are going to be baptized, ain't you, Buster?

BUSTER

You was going to tell me about what happened to Paul, remember? I . . .

(*Water is poured.*)

. . . well, after that I'll tell you my decision.

160

OCIE

All right. That's fair and square. It took some doing to get a nice tub like that one yonder—took some arranging—but I said, if a man was to decide he was going to be baptized, then the best wouldn't be none too good for him. The very best would be just barely good enough.

(*Water is poured.*)

BUSTER

How did he die, Preacher?

(*Water is poured.*)

OCIE

How did he die? Well, they trumped up this charge against him in Rome.

BUSTER

He was framed! Them sapsucking bastards, I might have knowed they'd have to frame him!

OCIE

Oh, it was dirty doings, all right. So they handed down this verdict, which was . . . to throw Paul to the tigers and lions . . .

(*Water is poured.*)

. . . down in a hole full of big cats!

BUSTER

And did he take it all right?

(*Water is poured.*)

OCIE

Never batted an eyelash. Paul was the sort of fellow that nothing fazed him. He knew who he was and where he was going. And when they . . . when they

161

come and got him out of his cell, they didn't have to
put ropes on him and drag him.

BUSTER

Walked right along by his *own self,* didn't he? I knew
he'd have acted that way!

OCIE

He had done already been baptized, of course, and he
knew there wasn't nothing to fear. He believed in
Jesus Christ, and he knew right where he was going.

BUSTER

And then what?

OCIE

So . . . so they got him to the edge of the pit where they
kept those hungry cats, and they was getting ready
to push him, and he says, "Just hold on a minute,
boys! There won't hardly be any need for that." He
wouldn't let them push him.

BUSTER

He didn't want them to, did he? They didn't have to
push him.

OCIE

That's right. He looked down . . .

(*Water is poured.*)

. . . he looked them lions and tigers right in the eye.
They was roaring and snarling. And then—he jumped.

BUSTER

I knew it. I knew he had to have gone out something
like that there. He went . . .

(*Water is poured.*)

. . . under his own steam, without nobody pushing and
shoving at him.

162

OCIE

I got something here he wrote. I'll read it to you.

BUSTER

All right. All right, let's hear it.

(*Water is poured.*)

OCIE (*Reading from the Bible*)

"Set your affection on things above, not on things on the earth. For ye are dead, and your life is hid with Christ in God. When Christ, who is our life, shall appear, then shall ye also appear with him in glory."

BUSTER

How could you know how I feel, Preacher—the awful things I done, the sins I committed? I'm all jammed up inside my chest . . .

(*Water is poured.*)

I feel so awful. I . . .

OCIE

It's the Holy Spirit, taking over your innards, wrapping up your soul!

BUSTER

What was that last you read—the last part, ". . . then shall ye . . ."?

OCIE

"Then shall ye also appear with him in glory."

BUSTER

Preacher, did Paul . . . did he mean me when he wrote that there?

OCIE

He sure did. That's the good news.

BUSTER

But I don't deserve it. I robbed. I killed. I murdered.

163

OCIE

Don't none . . .

(*Water is poured.*)

. . . don't nobody deserve it, Buster. I been meaning to ask—you got any folks, any kin?

BUSTER

Me? Naw, Preacher. It's like this here. There won't be nobody to write. There won't be nobody to notify. Nobody would claim me.

OCIE

I just thought that . . . well, maybe you had a sister or something.

BUSTER

A sister? Yeah, I had a sister, but I lost track of her long ago. We was orphaned, and Sis . . . well, she tried to look out for me. She was older. You know, I'd nearly forgot about her. Her given name was Sadie. They said she looked like our maw. Her hair was kind of red, like a peach pit. She was sure a good thing to me, Sadie was. But even . . . even if you could find her, I wouldn't want her to know nothing until after . . .

(*Water is poured.*)

. . . after it was all over with—a long time over with. I sure do miss her right now, my sis. I'll never see her again on this earth.

OCIE

Yeah.

(*Water is poured.*)

I know how you feel.

164

BYSTANDER

I believe that ought to be deep enough now, boys.

FATE

Your tub's ready, Preacher.

BUSTER

And I miss Paul. I ain't never got over seeing him shot that day. It was hot summer—him shot, laying there with his eyes open to the gnats—him dead and them revenue men opening up on all sides—out of every thicket and clump of cane . . .

BYSTANDER

If you don't mind, Deputy, me and some of the rest of the bunch would like to stay in here and watch the baptizing.

(*Ocie is fearful as Fate hesitates before answering.*)

FATE

I know how you feel, fellow. But . . . naw, I guess we better clear out. This unlocks the cell door.

(*He hands Ocie the key.*)

BYSTANDER

We'll be waiting outside, Preacher. Tell us when it's . . . it's over?

OCIE

I will.

BYSTANDER (*Pausing on his way out*)

Ah . . . Preacher . . . for the rest of the boys out yonder, for how we acted, I'm sorry. I want to say, we ain't none of us bad fellows at heart. I'm . . . I'm proud to know a real man of God. Just proud.

165

(He leaves. Ocie and Buster are locked inside the jail, alone together. Ocie unlocks Buster's cell and leads him out.)

BUSTER *(Hesitating)*

Wait a second. Wait.

OCIE

Just come this way, brother! This way!

(Buster holds back.)

BUSTER

Something I want to say. I got a confession, sort of. What I mean . . . before—you remember, Preacher? —when I hollered at that window and cussed the world. Well, I'm going to tell you something. I went to that window because . . . well, because really I was *scared*. I got so afraid thinking about when they were going to draw up that noose around my neck . . .

(He pauses.)

Well, time, what time there was left, would take me by the throat and . . . and it would seem to strangle me! The end—you don't know how dizzy and weak it would make me, just thinking about that morning. I'd see the mists, feel the damp and the cold. It begins to grey over in the east yonder—then the sun stabs over the hill, and you see how green all the leaves are, and you know it's the last day you'll be alive.

OCIE

I know, Brother. I know.

BUSTER

But Preacher, it's tomorrow—tomorrow when I'll wake

166

up and go look out that window the very last time. I won't be afraid. Not now. I'll know that you'll be out in that crowd, that you'll be by me when I walk out. And I'll hold my head up like a man. Be a man like Paul. It gives me strength because you believe like I do, because I can depend on you. Truly, Preacher, I ain't afraid no more.

(*He steps into the tub.*)

OCIE

Guess you better kneel down. I'll need a pretty good grip on you.

BUSTER

Do a good job, Preacher.

OCIE

I baptize thee in the name of the Father, and of the Son, and of the Holy Ghost.

BUSTER

"Then shall ye also appear with him in glory."

OCIE

Amen!

(*The seconds pass. After a minute, Ocie, at first intent on the murder, begins to tremble. A sob escapes him, and he hauls Buster up. Buster is strangling, coughing, half drowned.*)

BUSTER

You sure took me at my word when I said do a good job of it! I thought for a minute . . .

(*He pauses, suddenly realizing Ocie's intention.*)

You meant to drown me, didn't you, Preacher?

167

OCIE

I'll have to tell you. I'm Ocie Hedgepath. I never was
no preacher—just a bum is all.

BUSTER

Hedgepath. One of them?

OCIE

It was my sister, Kathleen, and her little chap.

BUSTER

It was your sister . . . with the baby—them. You going
to be there tomorrow, Preacher?

OCIE

Yeah, I'll be there.

(*He locks Buster back in his cell. The scrim wall appears, and Buster comes to the window. Dan, Rance,
and the Preacher have appeared at the edge of the
mob. Mary is there.*)

MOB LEADER

There stands Buster Drumwright, with the glory of
God's forgiveness dripping off him!

(*Fate lets Ocie out the security door at right and then
starts to lock it. As Ocie comes off the porch, Dan meets
him and springs on him with a sudden, violent cry.
Ocie turns, and Dan hugs him and draws a knife across
Ocie's middle, cutting him to the "hollow." Ocie sags
and falls.*)

MARY

No!

BUSTER

No! Not him! Not him! Me! Me! He's cut! He's cut!

168

DAN

Ocie, why'd you fail us—your own flesh—why!
(*Rance covers Fate with his gun.*)

RANCE

Run, Dan. Git! Don't come back. All right, Stanhope, get out of my way! I'm going in after him.
(*Dan flings down the knife and runs away as Rance starts to force his way past Fate into the jail. Mary rises from Ocie's side and falls on Rance's gun. Fate springs forward and disarms Rance.*)

FATE

Now you git! Cut down a *preacher*—you're *all* gone crazy!

MARY

You wanted blood, Rance! Here! Here!
(*Rance retreats before her bloody hands.*)
Cut to the hollow—your own brother! Dying!

RANCE

It was taking that tub—it was his idea we had to steal it. I knowed, from the first minute we laid a hand to it . . .

FATE

You better go, Rance. It's . . . he's a Hedgepath?—the Preacher?
(*Rance withdraws offstage.*)

PREACHER

Their lost brother, come home—to this.

MARY

Do something. He's dying!

169

MOB LEADER

Blood's pouring out of him. Better do something quick! Dan Hedgepath cut this preacher down . . .

OCIE

Rance! Rance! Is Rance gone?

PREACHER

He's gone.

OCIE

Dan? Dan . . . I don't blame you none. Is it you, Dan?

MARY

Somebody stop him. It's all spilling—bleeding . . .

OCIE

No. It's too late. Dan, it's all right. I feel dizzy—light-headed. Dan? Dan?

MOB MEMBER

Deputy, water's running out in the street yonder in front of Mr. Turner's house. Figured you . . . figured somebody . . . ought to be told.

FATE

All right, fellow. All right.

MOB MEMBER

Flooding the street. . . . Is he hurt much? Is he?

PREACHER

I knew when I saw Buster Drumwright alive at that window, I said, Ocie must not come out here. I said, they'll kill him. Well, they have!

MARY

You trying to say something, Ocie? Ocie?

OCIE

Just let me explain a minute, Dan. Rance—you, Rance?

170

PREACHER

They're here, Ocie. Go on.
(*He looks around, sees that Dan and Rance are gone.*)

OCIE

Can't see nothing. I'm . . . blind. It's so . . . dark.

PREACHER

Go on . . . Ocie.

OCIE

I had him . . . had him all the way under, like we planned. The power was pouring through my arms, all the power and vengeance—but, but it was . . . my arms shorted out on me. It come . . . him in yonder, *he* believed, and me . . . so did I believe too. I believed. The same as him, the same as Paul—so my arms, they shorted out on me, and I couldn't . . . you, Dan, and Rance . . . remember long ago . . . Dan?
(*He dies.*)

PREACHER

He's gone.

BUSTER

Why! Why him? Why not me? Why him?

MARY

I never knew him.

PREACHER

Who did? Who would have guessed in a thousand years what he was—on the inside?
(*He picks up the knife.*)

MARY

Never even knew him.
(*She begins sobbing quietly.*)

PREACHER

We better take him home.

MOB LEADER

Get a door. It's the best—a door's always the best. Take one off the hinges.

(*They bring a door and put Ocie on it. Fate has brought a blanket from the jail. They cover Ocie and bear him away. Mary, still sobbing, presses against the Preacher's side as they leave, following. The jail dims outside; the scrim wall fades as Fate goes into the cell block, carrying a stool and his checkerboard. Buster comes from the window.*)

BUSTER

Why him?

FATE

Tomorrow's the day! Want to play checkers? Maybe get your mind off—all this—off tomorrow? I'll set up the board . . .

BUSTER

You think he knew they'd kill him when he went out there just now? Remember how he went . . . just right on out, and he knew! He *knew*. Didn't he?

FATE

Why not? Sure he knew. Sure.

BUSTER

And he was going to be with me tomorrow. He said so.

FATE

Well, he will be. You'll be going to the same place where he's at now.

172

(*The banjo begins softly playing* MANSIONS IN THE SKIES.)

BUSTER

He was going to be with me out there every last step of the way. You know, he was the real kind—he come to believing the hard way, like every last suffering bastard before him—come to it hard, like Paul done. Oh, he might have been throwed in jail now and then—he might have had some of that all right. Don't I know? I seen a long time that only the best and the worst gets throwed in jail. The middle folks—*the easy believers*—run free. He'll be around—hell yes, he will. I know him. I know his kind. No sorrow, nothing you can do would ever bust that fellow away from the Lord's work. Bust his back, mash his heart—kill him—still he'll keep going. He's up there now somewhere, standing on some rundown street corner, down in the slums where it's only drunks and homeless dishwashers, louse-den operators, tired old whores. But he's there preaching, comforting, converting. I . . . I'll know where to find him all right.

FATE

Want me to set up the checkerboard?

BUSTER

Not tonight, fellow. You know, since that first son of a bitch ever I killed, three years ago, I ain't had one good night's rest? Well . . . I'm gonna sleep now.

FATE

Have it your way.

173

(Jail dims out as Ralph Swiggert comes down center stage, still playing. Ralph sings.)

RALPH

"When I can read my title clear to mansions in the skies,
I'll bid farewell to earthly joys and wipe my weepin'
eyes.
Oh, I feel like, I feel like, I'm on my journey home;
I feel like, I feel like, I'm on my journey home."

(Still strumming the minor-key melody, he turns and goes up center stage, a minstrel silhouette against a blood-red sky.)

[THE END]

COLOPHON

THE TEXT of this book is set in twelve-point Granjon, two points leaded. This type face was designed for the Linotype by G. W. Jones and named for Robert Granjon, a great sixteenth-century French type founder and printer, although it actually bears a close resemblance to and is based on the types cut by Claude Garamond, another French printer of the sixteenth century. It is an elegant face, with tall ascenders, and is highly legible, even in small sizes. The title page and display matter are set in several sizes of Caslon Old Style. These designs were cut early in the eighteenth century by William Caslon, the greatest English type founder. Modeled on Dutch types of the seventeenth century, Caslon's designs far surpass their originals in interest, delicacy, and variety.

The book is printed on Warren's Olde Style paper, manufactured by the S. D. Warren Company, of Boston, and is bound in a cloth manufactured by the Arkwright-Interlaken Company, of Fiskeville, Rhode Island. Composition, printing, and binding were done by the Parthenon Press, of Nashville. The typography and binding design are by Paul Randall Mize.